CliffsNotes®
Writing: Grammar, Usage, and Style Quick Review

CliffsNotes®
Writing: Grammar, Usage, and Style Quick Review

By Jean Eggenschwiler, M.A., Emily Dotson Biggs, and Claudia L. W. Reinhardt

3rd Edition

Houghton Mifflin Harcourt
Boston • New York

About the Authors

Jean Eggenschwiler, M.A. is a graduate of U.C. Berkeley and Stanford University. She has taught English and Composition in high school and worked as a business editor and writer.

Emily Dotson Biggs has been an adjunct instructor at Paducah Community College and Murray State University and has taught English to students from kindergarten to college.

Claudia L. W. Reinhardt holds degrees from Illinois Wesleyan University and Emerson College. She has worked as a writer and editor in business communications, and now teaches in the Writing Center at Southeast Community College.

Publisher's Acknowledgments

Editorial

Acquisitions Editor: Greg Tubach

Project Editor: Lynn Northrup

Technical Editor: Barbara Swovelin

Composition

Indexer: Potomac Indexing, LLC

Proofreader: Shannon Ramsey

Wiley Publishing, Inc. Composition Services

Copyright © 2013 by Houghton Mifflin Harcourt Publishing Company
All rights reserved

www.hmhco.com

Library of Congress Cataloging-in-Publication data is available.
ISBN 978-0-470-88078-4 (pbk)

Printed in the United States of America
DOC 10 9 8 7
4500477976

Table of Contents

Introduction

Effective writing is an essential communication skill that is necessary in personal relationships and in almost every profession. Fortunately, writing is a skill you can learn! Whether you are a high school or college student, a business professional, or just someone interested in improving your written communication, this book will help you become a better writer. It is organized to be useful to both the beginner and experienced writer.

This book provides an easy-to-follow, practical guide to the fundamentals of writing, including information about grammar, sentences, punctuation, words, and the writing process. First, you review the basic rules of grammar, including the parts of speech and their usage. Next, you see how phrases, clauses, and sentences are constructed, and you learn tips on avoiding some of the basic errors in constructing sentences. Then, you discover how to take the mystery out of punctuation rules, including frustrating comma decisions. After this, you explore word choice and usage, and are given helpful suggestions for avoiding common problems that can occur when choosing words. Finally, in a simple step-by-step guide, you learn how to go through the process that leads to good writing.

How This Book Will Help You

Can you answer yes to any of these questions?

- Do you need to review the fundamentals of grammar?
- Do you want to know how to write better?
- Do you want to effectively communicate your ideas in writing?
- Do you need a supplement to English courses?
- Do you need to prepare for a test that evaluates writing skills?
- Do you need a concise, comprehensive reference for grammar and writing?
- Is effective writing important in your job or personal life?

If so, *CliffsNotes Writing: Grammar, Usage, and Style Quick Review, 3rd Edition*, is for you!

How to Use This Book

You can use this book in any way that fits your personal style for study and review. You decide what works best for your needs. You can either read the book from cover to cover, or just look for the information as you need it. Here are just a few ways you can search for topics:

- Look for areas of interest in the book's Table of Contents, or use the index to find specific topics.

- Read the book and look for your topic in the running heads.

- Look in the Glossary for important terms and definitions.

- Get a glimpse of what you'll gain from a chapter by scanning the "Chapter Check-In" at the beginning of each chapter.

- Test your knowledge in the Chapter Check-Out quizzes or Review Questions.

- Discover additional information in the Resource Center.

- Skim the book for special terms in bold type.

- Flip through the book until you find what you're looking for.

Hundreds of Practice Questions Online!

Prepare for your next Writing quiz or test with hundreds of additional practice questions online. The questions are organized by this book's chapter sections, so it's easy to use the book and then quiz yourself online to make sure you know the subject. Go to www.cliffsnotes.com/go/quiz/writing to test yourself anytime and find other free homework help.

Chapter 1

NOUN: PERSON, PLACE, THING, IDEA, OR ACTIVITY

Chapter Check-In

❏ Identify proper nouns and gerunds

❏ Use collective nouns to identify groups

❏ Understand singular and plural nouns

❏ Use possessive nouns to show ownership

❏ Make nouns and verbs agree

A noun is a part of speech that names a person, place, thing, idea, or activity. Some nouns are specific for people, places, or events; and some represent groups or collections. Some nouns aren't even technically labeled nouns as their part of speech; they're verbs acting like nouns in sentences.

Nouns can be singular, referring to one thing, or plural, referring to more than one thing. Nouns can be possessive, indicating ownership or a close relationship. Regardless of the type, nouns should always agree with their verbs in sentences. Use singular verbs with singular nouns and plural verbs with plural nouns. You have to know how a noun works in order to write an effective sentence.

Proper Nouns

If a noun names a specific person or place, or a particular event or group, it is called a **proper noun** and is always capitalized. Some examples are *Eleanor Roosevelt, Niagara Falls, Dracula, the Federal Bureau of Investigation, the Great Depression.*

Unfortunately, some writers assign proper-noun status indiscriminately to words, sprinkling capital letters freely throughout their writing. For example, the *Manhattan Project* is correctly capitalized because it is a historic project, the name given to the specific wartime effort to design and build the first nuclear weapons. But the common noun *project* should not be capitalized when referring to a club's project to clean up the campus, for example. Similarly, the *Great Depression* should be capitalized because it refers to the specific period of economic failure that began with the stock market collapse in 1929. When the word *depression* refers to other economic hard times, however, it is not a proper noun; it is a common noun and should not be capitalized.

Some flexibility in capitalizing nouns is acceptable. A writer may have a valid reason for capitalizing a particular term. For example, some companies have style guides that dictate capital letters for job titles such as *manager*. But often the capitalization beyond the basic guidelines is an effort to give a word an air of importance, and you should avoid it.

Verbs Used as Nouns

Sometimes in English, a verb is used as a noun. When the verb form is altered and it serves the same function as a noun in the sentence, it is called a **gerund.**

Gerunds

A noun created from the *-ing* form of a verb can act as a subject or an object in a sentence.

> *Sleeping* sometimes serves as an escape from *studying*.

The gerunds *sleeping* and *studying* are *-ing* forms of the verbs *sleep* and *study*. *Sleeping* is a noun functioning as the subject of this sentence, and *studying* is a noun functioning as an object (in this case, the object of a preposition; see Chapter 5, "Connecting Words and Phrases: Prepositions, Conjunctions, and Interjections").

Problem gerunds

Gerunds can sometimes be difficult to use correctly in a sentence. What problems can you have with gerunds?

When a noun or pronoun precedes a gerund, use the possessive case of the noun or pronoun. (For the possessive case of the pronoun, see Chapter 3, "Pronoun: Word Used in Place of a Noun.")

Jana's sleeping was sometimes an escape from studying.

To test for correct usage, substitute the noun in place of the gerund. For example, in the preceding sentence, replace the gerund *sleeping* with the noun *slumber.* Read these sentences aloud and listen for the difference.

Jana's slumber was sometimes an escape from studying.

NOT *Jana slumber* was sometimes an escape from studying.

Even when you think that the word before the gerund looks like an object, use the possessive case.

Jana was annoyed by *Bill's studying.*

NOT Jana was annoyed by *Bill studying.*

Collective Nouns

A word that stands for a group of things is called a **collective noun.** In fact, the word *group* itself is a collective noun. Here are a few others: *family, club, team, committee, staff, furniture, jury, Congress, audience, herd.*

Usually these nouns are treated as singular because the emphasis is on the action of the entire unit rather than its individual parts.

The *team is* going on the bus.

The *committee wants* to find a solution to the problem.

But when you want to emphasize the individual parts of a group, you may treat a collective noun as plural.

The *team have* argued about going on the bus.

The *committee want* different solutions to the problem.

If the plural sounds awkward, try rewording.

The *team members have* argued about going on the bus.

The *committee members want* different solutions to the problem.

Singular and Plural Nouns

The term **number** refers to whether a noun is singular or plural. Most nouns can be either singular or plural, depending on whether you are talking about one thing or more than one. You know the basic rule of adding *-s* to make the plural of a noun (*one cat, three cats*), and you also know that many nouns don't follow that rule—for example, *sheep* (singular), *sheep* (plural); *enemy, enemies; wharf, wharves; hero, heroes; goose, geese*, and so on. Check a dictionary if you're not sure how to spell a plural noun. Do not add an apostrophe + *s* to a singular form to make it plural, even if the noun is a family name: *the Taylors*, not *the Taylor's; donkeys*, not *donkey's; taxis*, not *taxi's*.

The singular and plural forms of some nouns with Latin and Greek endings can cause trouble. The noun *data*, for example, is plural; *datum* is the singular form. Although today the plural *data* is widely used as a singular noun, you should keep the distinction, particularly in scientific writing.

> The final *datum* (singular) is not consistent with the preceding *data* (plural), which *are* positive.

Here are some examples of Latin and Greek singular and plural words that can be troublesome: *bacterium, bacteria; criterion, criteria; medium, media; alumnus* (masculine singular), *alumni* (masculine plural), *alumna* (feminine singular), *alumnae* (feminine plural).

Possessive Case of Nouns

The **possessive case** of a noun is used to show ownership (*Jordan's car, my sister's house*) or other close relationship (*the president's friends, the university's position*).

Problems with possessives

Sometimes possessives can cause problems. Do I add an *'s* or just an apostrophe? Follow this rule: For singular nouns, add *'s*, even if the noun ends in an *-s* or *-z* sound: *dog's, house's, Wes's, Jesus's, Denver's, Keats's*.

For most plural possessive nouns, add an apostrophe alone: *several months' bills, many Romanians' apartments, the encyclopedias' differences*. If a plural noun doesn't end in *-s*, add *-'s*, just as you would with a singular noun: *women's issues, mice's tails*.

Switching to an *of* construction

When a possessive noun sounds awkward, reword to use an *of* construction. This is a better way to indicate the relationship, especially when referring to an inanimate object: *the top of the page* instead of *the page's top; the lawn of the building on the corner* instead of *the building on the corner's lawn; the main characters of* Pride and Prejudice instead of Pride and Prejudice's *main characters; the novels of Dickens* instead of *Dickens's novels.*

Joint ownership

One last word about possessive nouns: When you are indicating joint ownership, use the possessive form in the final name only, such as *Abbott and Costello's movies; Tom and Dawn's dinner party; Smith, Wilson, and Nelson's partnership.*

Agreement of Nouns and Verbs

Agreement is an important concept in grammar and a source of many writing errors. It will come up again under pronouns (Chapter 3) and under sentence construction (Chapter 7, "Common Sentence Errors").

Nouns must agree with their verbs, which means that a singular noun requires a singular verb, and a plural noun requires a plural verb.

> The *rabbit jumps* up and down. (singular)
> The *rabbits jump* up and down. (plural)

Remember that a noun ending in *-s* is often a plural, whereas a verb ending in *-s* is usually singular: four *home runs* (plural noun); he *runs fast* (singular verb).

Nouns with Latin or Greek endings and nouns that look plural but sometimes take singular verbs can cause agreement problems.

In the following example, *criteria* is plural. Use the plural form of the verb (*are*).

> The *criteria* for judging an entry *are* listed in the brochure.

Rights, which is a plural form, is treated as singular in the following example because *human rights* is a unit, a single issue of concern.

> *Human rights is* an issue that affects everyone.

To emphasize the rights individually, use the plural verb.

Human rights are ignored in many countries.

In the next example, *miles* is the plural form, but *fifty miles* is used to identify a single unit of distance and therefore takes a singular verb.

Fifty miles is not such a long distance.

Statistics looks plural, and in many situations is treated as plural. In the first example below, *statistics* refers to a subject of study, so the singular verb is appropriate.

Statistics is a subject I want to avoid.

Statistics are being gathered to show that women are better drivers than men.

Among other frequently used nouns that can take either a singular or plural verb, depending on whether the emphasis is on a single unit or individual items, are *number, majority,* and *minority.*

The *number* of people coming *is* surprising.

A *number* of people *are* coming.

A *number* like five thousand *is* what he had in mind.

With *number,* use this rule. If *number* is preceded by *the,* always use the singular verb. If *number* is preceded by *a,* use the singular or plural, depending on whether you are describing a single unit or individual items.

With *majority* and *minority,* the key is to decide whether you want to emphasize individual people or things or the single unit.

The *majority is* opposed to the measure. (singular = single unit)

A *minority* of the younger people *refuse* to concede the point. (plural = individuals)

Chapter Check-Out

Questions

1. Identify the underlined nouns in the following sentences as common or proper nouns.

   a. Dylan plans to go to <u>college</u> in the fall.
   b. Sara was accepted to <u>Watson College</u>.

2. Identify the underlined nouns in the following sentences as a collective noun, singular noun, or a gerund.

   a. The <u>commission</u> plans to review the report.
   b. <u>Running</u> is fun.
   c. My <u>coach</u> is great.
   d. The <u>company</u> established a strict dress code.

3. Match the underlined nouns with the corresponding term that best describes the type of noun.

   a. My <u>dog's</u> bone was lost.   singular noun
   b. The <u>women</u> meet for lunch.   singular possessive noun
   c. My <u>sons'</u> cars need to be washed. plural noun
   d. A <u>girl</u> lost her scarf on the bus. plural possessive noun

4. Fill in the blank with the correct form of the verb to make the noun and verb agree in the following sentences.

   a. Margaret and Tommy _____ happy. (look, looks)
   b. John, as well as Ali and Griffin, _____ to visit Orlando. (plan, plans)
   c. Many components of the company's computer system_____ badly outmoded. (are, is)
   d. The danger of scuba diving _____ not discourage Lily. (do, does)
   e. While wearing her school uniform, Tessie _____ for charity. (dance, dances)

Answers

1. a. common; **b.** proper

2. a. collective; **b.** gerund; **c.** singular; **d.** collective

3. a. singular possessive; **b.** plural; **c.** plural possessive; **d.** singular

4. a. look; **b.** plans; **c.** are; **d.** does; **e.** dances

Chapter 2

VERB: WORD OR PHRASE EXPRESSING ACTION OR STATE OF BEING

Chapter Check-In

❑ Identify action and linking verbs

❑ Understand active voice and passive voice

❑ Recognize transitive and intransitive verbs

❑ Use common verb tenses

❑ Correct common verb problems

A verb is a part of speech that expresses action or state of being, or connects a subject to a complement. Verbs indicate whether the subject performs an action (active voice) or receives the action (passive voice). Verbs can be transitive (requires a direct object) or intransitive (does not require an object). The tenses of verbs are formed according to person, number, and tense.

Verbs can have moods, which indicate the attitude of the speaker. Some writers have problems with verbs as the result of an incorrect tense or irregular verbs. Verbs play a key role in constructing sentences.

Action Verbs and Linking Verbs

An **action verb** animates a sentence, either physically (*swim, jump, drop, whistle*) or mentally (*think, dream, believe, suppose, love*). Verbs make sentences move; sometimes dramatically, sometimes quietly.

She *leaped* high into the air, *twirled, landed* on the floor, and *ran* from the room.

He *thought* of her beauty, *imagined* her smile, *yearned* for her presence.

Some verbs don't express action but help complete statements about the subject by describing or identifying it. These verbs are called **linking verbs.**

Diane *is* happy.

Clement *feels* feverish.

Maria *is* a doctor.

The music *sounds* good.

The sentences don't tell you what Diane, Clement, Maria, and the music *did* but rather what they *are.* Linking verbs "link" their subjects to a classification, state of being, or quality. In the sentences above, *happy, feverish, doctor,* and *good* are called **complements** of the linking verbs. (See Chapter 3, "Pronoun: Word Used in Place of a Noun.") Table 2-1 lists some common linking verbs.

Table 2-1   Common Linking Verbs

appear	grow	smell
be	look	sound
become	remain	taste
feel	seem	

Some of these verbs can be both linking and action verbs.

Clement *felt* hot. (linking verb)
Clement *felt* along the wall for the light switch. (action verb)

The dog *smelled* bad. (linking verb)
The dog *smelled* the man's boots. (action verb)

A quick way to tell whether a verb is functioning as a linking verb is to see if you can replace it with a form of the verb *to be* and still have a logical sentence. For example, test the two sentences above by replacing *smelled* with *was.*

The dog *was* bad. (yes)

The dog *was* the man's boots. (no)

Linking verbs operate differently than action verbs. First, while action verbs are modified by adverbs, linking verbs are often followed by adjectives.

This cheese *smells strong*.

NOT This cheese *smells strongly*.

This rule is discussed in Chapter 4, "Modifiers: Adjectives, Adverbs, and Compound Modifiers."

Also, a pronoun following the linking verb *to be* should be in the subjective case rather than the objective case.

It *was she*.

NOT It *was her*.

This rule is discussed in Chapter 3.

Active Voice and Passive Voice

The term **voice** refers to the form of a verb indicating whether the subject performs an action (**active voice**) or receives the action (**passive voice**).

Marcy *smashed* the ball over the net. (active voice)

The ball *was smashed* over the net by Marcy. (passive voice)

Use the active voice whenever you can because it conveys more energy than the passive voice and results in more concise writing. (See Chapter 6, "Phrases, Clauses, and Sentences.")

Use the passive voice when you don't know who is taking the action (actor), when you don't want to name the actor, or when you want to emphasize the person or thing acted upon rather than the one taking the action. The passive voice is often appropriate in scientific writing.

When we returned, the *car had been towed*.

I regret that a *mistake was made*.

Gold was discovered in California.

His *mother was rushed* to the hospital.

A *change* in structure *was found* in the experimental group.

Transitive and Intransitive Verbs

A transitive verb, used with a direct object, transmits action to an object and may also have an indirect object, which indicates to or for whom the action is done. In contrast, an intransitive verb never takes an object.

Transitive verbs

A **transitive verb** takes a **direct object;** that is, the verb transmits action to an object.

> He *sent* the *letter.* (*letter* = direct object of *sent*)
>
> She *gave* the *lecture.* (*lecture* = direct object of *gave*)

In these sentences, something is being done to an object.

A transitive verb can also have an **indirect object** that precedes the direct object. The indirect object tells to or for whom the action is done, although the words *to* and *for* are not used. In the following examples, notice the difference between the direct and indirect objects.

The direct object (*letter*) receives the action (*sent*). The indirect object (*Robert*) is the person to whom the letter is sent.

> He *sent Robert* the *letter.*

The direct object (*lecture*) receives the action (*gave*). The indirect object (*class*) is the group to whom the lecture is given.

> She *gave* her *class* the lecture.

Learn to recognize words that are direct and indirect objects of verbs. When these words are pronouns, they must be in the objective case. See Chapter 3 for an explanation of pronoun cases.

Intransitive verbs

An **intransitive verb** does not take an object.

> She *sleeps* too much.
>
> He *complains* frequently.

In these sentences, nothing receives the action of the verbs *sleep* and *complain.*

Many verbs can be either transitive or intransitive.

> She *sings* every day. (no object = intransitive)
>
> She *sings rock 'n' roll tunes.* (*rock 'n' roll tunes* receives the action of *sings* = transitive)

Verbals: Gerunds, Infinitives, and Participles

The three verbals—**gerunds, infinitives,** and **participles**—are formed from verbs, but are never used alone as action words in sentences. Instead, verbals function as nouns, adjectives, or adverbs. These verbals are important in phrases (discussed in Chapter 6).

The **gerund** (see Chapter 1, "Noun: Person, Place, Thing, Idea, or Activity") ends in *-ing* and functions as a noun.

> *Jumping* is fun.
>
> He liked *skiing.*
>
> He had a unique way of *whistling.*

The **infinitive** is the base form of a verb with *to.* Usually it functions as a noun, although it can also function as an adjective or adverb.

> *To jump* is fun. (noun; subject of the verb *is*)
>
> I like *to ski.* (noun; direct object of the verb *like*)
>
> She had a suggestion *to offer.* (adjective modifying *suggestion*)
>
> He called *to warn* her. (adverb modifying the verb *called*)

A **participle** is a verb that ends in *-ing* (present participle) or *-ed, -d, -t, -en, -n* (past participle). Participles may function as adjectives, describing or modifying nouns.

> The *dancing* parrots entertained the crowd.
>
> The *wrecked* sailboat washed up on shore.

But participles have another function. When used with helping verbs such as *to be* and *to have,* they are action verbs and form several verb **tenses.**

> She *is thinking* of the children.
>
> The conference room *had been cleaned* before they arrived.

Forming Verb Tenses

To write correctly, you need to know both how to form verb tenses and when to use them. Verb tenses are formed according to person, number, and tense. They are the key to coherent sentence structure.

Tense, person, and number

Person refers to the subject or object of the verb. Number identifies whether a verb is singular or plural. A few terms will help you to understand how verb tenses are formed.

- **Tense:** Refers to the time the action (or state of being) is taking place

- **Number:** Refers to whether a verb is singular (*he goes*) or plural (*they go*)

    In the sentence *The horse runs in the pasture,* the verb *runs* is the third-person singular of the present tense of the verb *run*.

- **Person:** Refers to the person (or thing) that is a subject or object

    First person: *I go* (singular). *We go* (plural). *She spoke to me* (singular). *She spoke to us* (singular subject).

    Second person: *You go* (singular). *You (all) go* (plural). *She spoke to you, you (all)* (singular subject).

    Third person: *He, She, It goes* (singular). *They go* (plural). *She spoke to him, her, it* (singular). *She spoke to them* (singular subject, plural object).

Common verb tenses

Here are the most commonly used tenses in English:

- **Present:** Action going on now
- **Past:** Action that is completed
- **Future:** Action that has yet to take place
- **Present perfect:** Action in past time in relation to present time
- **Past perfect:** Action in past time in relation to another past time
- **Future perfect:** Action in a future time in relation to another time farther in the future

Definitions of the perfect tenses are difficult to understand without examples. Tables 2-2 through 2-7 show the regular verb *to walk* and the irregular verb *to be* in each of the tenses for first-, second-, and third-person subjects. Regular verbs, like *to walk,* form the past tense and the perfect tenses by adding *-d* or *-ed* to the present tense. But many English verbs are irregular, forming their past tenses in various ways. A list of frequently used irregular verbs is provided at the end of the chapter.

Table 2-2   Present Tense

	Singular	*Plural*
First person	I walk	we walk
	I am	we are
Second person	you walk	you walk
	you are	you are
Third person	he, she, it walked	they walk
	he, she, it is	they are

Table 2-3   Past Tense

	Singular	*Plural*
First person	I walked	we walked
	I was	we were
Second person	you walked	you walked
	you were	you were
Third person	he, she, it walked	they walked
	he, she, it was	they were

Table 2-4   Future Tense

	Singular	*Plural*
First person	I will walk	we will walk
	I will be	we will be
Second person	you will walk	you will walk
	you will be	you will be
Third person	he, she, it will walk	they will walk
	he, she, it will be	they will be

In the future tense, traditionally *shall* has been used for *will* in the first-person singular and plural: I *shall* walk, we *shall* walk. In modern usage, *will* has replaced *shall* almost entirely. Although either is correct, *shall* can sound overly formal.

Table 2-5   Present Perfect Tense

	Singular	Plural
First person	I have walked	we have walked
	I have been	we have been
Second person	you have walked	you have walked
	you have been	you have been
Third person	he, she, it has walked	they have walked
	he, she, it has been	they have been

Table 2-6   Past Perfect Tense

	Singular	Plural
First person	I had walked	we had walked
	I had been	we had been
Second person	you had walked	you had walked
	you had been	you had been
Third person	he, she, it had walked	they had walked
	he, she, it had been	they had been

Table 2-7   Future Perfect Tense

	Singular	Plural
First person	I will have walked	we will have walked
	I will have been	we will have been
Second person	you will have walked	you will have walked
	you will have been	you will have been
Third person	he, she, it will have walked	they will have walked
	he, she, it will have been	they will have been

Using the Tenses

Tense indicates when the action or state of being occurs. Forming tenses can be simple or complicated.

Present, past, and future

The present, past, and future tenses are part of our everyday language, and as writers we should be able to use these forms with ease. The present tense indicates an action occurring now.

> He *calls* her on his cell phone every hour.

Sometimes, the present tense is used to indicate future action.

> Her plane *arrives* on Friday.

The past tense indicates action completed in the past.

> He *called* her on his cell phone yesterday.

The future tense is used for action that will occur at a future time.

> He *will call* her on his cell phone next week.

Present perfect

The present perfect tense, formed with *has* or *have* and the past participle of the verb, indicates an action that occurred in the past and has continued into the present.

> I *have called* you for a week. (And I am still calling you.)

This contrasts with the simple past tense, which suggests an action that both began and ended in the past.

> I *called* you for a week. (But I am no longer calling you.)

The present perfect tense can also be used when you want to emphasize an action that occurred in the past but at no definite time.

> I *have called* many times.

Past perfect

The past perfect tense, formed with *had* and the past participle of the verb, indicates an action completed in the past *before* another action completed in the past.

After I *had called* you ten times, I *checked* your phone number.

Had called is a past action that was completed *before* checking the phone number, another completed past action.

In the following example, his being sober for a year *preceded* the accident: past before past.

He *had been sober* for a year when the accident *happened*.

Future perfect

The future perfect tense, formed with *will have* and the past participle of the verb, is used for an action that will be completed in the future *before* another future action.

By next week, I *will have texted* you more than a hundred times.

Texting more than a hundred times will take place *before* next week. In the following example, his achieving sobriety for a year will *precede* the future arrival of his baby daughter.

He *will have been* sober for a year by the time his new daughter is born.

Moods of the Verb

Verb moods are classifications that indicate the attitude of the speaker. Verbs have three moods—indicative, imperative, and subjunctive.

Indicative and imperative moods

The indicative and the imperative moods are fairly common. You use the **indicative** mood in most statements and questions.

He *walks* every day after lunch.
Does he *believe* in the benefits of exercise?

You use the **imperative** in requests and commands. Imperative statements have an understood subject of "you" and therefore take second-person verbs.

Sit down. ([*You*] sit down.)

Please *take* a number. ([*You*] please take a number.)

Subjunctive mood

Verb tenses in the **subjunctive** mood are used in special kinds of statements. The most common use of the subjunctive mood is in contrary-to-fact or hypothetical statements. In your own writing, you must decide which statements should be in the subjunctive mood. If something is likely to happen, use the indicative. If something is hypothetical, or contrary to fact, use the subjunctive.

■ **Present tense subjunctive**

If I *were* king, you would be queen. (In the subjunctive, *were* is used for all persons.)

If he *worked,* he could earn high wages.

■ **Past tense subjunctive**

If I *had been* king, you would have been queen.

If he *had worked,* he could have earned high wages.

These contrary-to-fact statements have two clauses: the *if* clause and the consequences clause. The forms of the verbs in these clauses are different from those of verbs used in the indicative mood.

In the **if clause,** use the subjunctive. Table 2-8 shows how it is formed. Note that the subjunctive present tense is the same as the indicative past tense.

Table 2-8   Present Subjunctive

Verb to be: *were*	*If I were king, If he were king.*
Other verbs: *worked*	*If I worked, If he worked.*

Note in Table 2-9 how the subjunctive past tense is the same as the indicative past perfect tense.

Table 2-9   Past Subjunctive

Verb to be: *had been*	If I had been king, If he had been king.
Other verbs: *had worked*	If I had worked, If he had worked.

In the **consequences clause,** use the conditional (Tables 2-10 and 2-11), which is formed with *could* or *would.*

Table 2-10   Present Conditional

could, would + base form of verb	You would be queen.
	He could earn high wages.

Table 2-11   Past Conditional

could, would + have + past participle of verb	You would have been queen.
	He could have earned high wages.

Not all clauses beginning with *if* are contrary to fact. When an *if* clause indicates something that is *likely* to happen, use the indicative, not the subjunctive.

If I *study* hard [likely to happen], I *will pass* the test.

If his fever *continues* to fall [likely to happen], he *will recover.*

Problems with Verbs

Writers sometimes use an incorrect tense or don't know how to use the past participle forms of irregular verbs. Using verb tenses imprecisely or inconsistently can also distract a reader and block communication.

Illogical time sequence

Recognize time sequences in your writing and choose verb tenses that logically reflect that sequence. Sometimes the choice of a verb tense affects your meaning.

Kelsey *worked* at the library for a year.

As the previous sentence shows, the past tense indicates a completed action. Kelsey no longer works at the library.

Kelsey *has worked* at the library for a year.

Here, the present perfect tense indicates that a past action is continuing in the present. Kelsey is still working at the library.

Kelsey *had worked* at the library for a year.

In this sentence, the past perfect tense indicates that something else happened after Kelsey's year at the library. For example, Kelsey *had worked* at the library for a year when she was asked to take over technology development.

When to use the perfect tense

Learn to use the perfect tenses when they are appropriate to your meaning. Don't limit yourself to the simple past tense when writing about past action. In the following sentences, a perfect tense should have been used to establish a clear time sequence.

The car wash *stood* where the sandwich shop *was*. (no)

All the things you *told* me, I *heard* before. (no)

In the first sentence, since the sandwich shop was in the location before the car wash—they can't occupy the same space at the same time—past perfect should be used for the second verb.

The car wash *stood* where the sandwich shop *had been*.

The logic of the second sentence dictates that *heard* should be in the past perfect tense. The word *before* is an obvious clue that the hearing took place before the telling, even though both actions were completed in the past.

All the things you *told* me, I *had heard* before.

Faulty *if* clauses

The past perfect tense should also be used in a subjunctive past tense "*if* clause."

If she *had thought* of it, she would have called you.

A common error is to use the conditional *would have* or *could have* in both clauses. *Would have* and *could have* should be used *only* in the clause that states the consequences.

> If I *had wanted* to, I *would have* made cookies.
>
> NOT If I *would have wanted* to, I *would have* made cookies.

> If we *had brought* matches, we *could have* made a bonfire.
>
> NOT If we *would have brought* matches, we *could have* made a bonfire.

Inconsistency in tenses

Another common error is illogically mixing tenses in a sentence or in a piece of writing. Choose the verb tense you want to use in your sentence or in your essay. Then make sure that all verbs are consistent, either by being in the same tense or by reflecting past and future times in relation to your main tense.

> Roberto *went* into the market, *walks* over to the produce section, and *picks* through the tomatoes. (inconsistent tenses)

In the preceding sentence there is no logical reason to move from the past tense (*went*) to the present tense (*walks, picks*). Use the past tense or the present tense—not both. Rewrite the sentence using consistent tenses.

> Roberto *went* into the market, *walked* over to the produce section, and *picked* through the tomatoes. (consistent tenses)

Look at the verb tenses in this group of sentences.

> This new program *will pay* its own way. It *specified* that anyone who *wanted* to use the service *has to pay* a fee. People who *refused* to do so *won't* receive the benefits. (inconsistent tenses)

Notice that the changes in tense between sentences are not related to a clear time sequence. A rewritten version of this piece shows a more consistent, logical use of tenses.

> This new program *will pay* its own way. It *specifies* that anyone who *wants* to use the service *has to pay* a fee. People who *refuse* to do so *won't* receive the benefits. (consistent tenses)

In this version, all verb tenses except the first (*will pay*) and last (*won't receive = will not receive*) are in the present tense. The future tense is correctly used for the first and last verbs because these verbs indicate future consequences.

Irregular verbs

Even when you understand the correct uses of verb tenses, you can run into trouble with irregular verbs. Irregular verbs form the past tense and past participle in a variety of ways (as shown in Table 2-12), not by adding *-d* or *-ed* as regular verbs do.

Table 2-12   Tenses of Regular and Irregular Verbs

	Regular Verbs	*Irregular Verbs*
Present:	*talk, joke*	*say, bite*
Past:	*talked, joked*	*said, bit*
Past participle:	*have talked, have joked*	*have said, have bitten*

Irregular verbs cause errors because people aren't sure about the correct past and past participle forms. Which is it: "I *drunk* the beer" or "I *drank* the beer"? Table 2-13 is a list of common irregular verbs with their past tenses and past participles. However, there are many others, so when you aren't sure about a verb, check the dictionary. The entry will include the verb's principal parts: present, past, and past participle.

Table 2-13   Common Irregular Verbs

Present Tense	Past Tense	Past Participle
be	was, were	(have) been
beat	beat	(have) beaten, beat
begin	began	(have) begun
blow	blew	(have) blown
break	broke	(have) broken
bring	brought	(have) brought
catch	caught	(have) caught
choose	chose	(have) chosen
come	came	(have) come
dig	dug	(have) dug
dive	dived, dove	(have) dived
do	did	(have) done
draw	drew	(have) drawn
dream	dreamed, dreamt	(have) dreamed, dreamt
drink	drank	(have) drunk
drive	drove	(have) driven
eat	ate	(have) eaten
fly	flew	(have) flown
forget	forgot	(have) forgotten
freeze	froze	(have) frozen
get	got	(have) gotten
go	went	(have) gone
grow	grew	(have) grown
hang (an object)	hung	(have) hung
hang (a person)	hanged	(have) hanged
lay	laid	(have) laid
lead	led	(have) led
lend	lent	(have) lent
lie (recline)	lay	(have) lain

Present Tense	Past Tense	Past Participle
light	lighted, lit	(have) lighted, lit
ride	rode	(have) ridden
ring	rang	(have) rung
run	ran	(have) run
see	saw	(have) seen
set	set	(have) set
shake	shook	(have) shaken
shine (emit light)	shone	(have) shone
shine (make shiny)	shone, shined	(have) shone, shined
sing	sang	(have) sung
sink	sank, sunk	(have) sunk
slay	slew	(have) slain
speed	sped	(have) sped
spring	sprang, sprung	(have) sprung
steal	stole	(have) stolen
swear	swore	(have) sworn
swim	swam	(have) swum
take	took	(have) taken
tear	tore	(have) torn
wake	waked, woke	(have) waked, woke, woken
wear	wore	(have) worn

Chapter Check-Out

Questions

1. Identify the following verbs as active or passive voice.

   a. The song <u>was sung</u> by my favorite group.
   b. She <u>took</u> the exam last week.
   c. *Beloved* <u>was written</u> by Toni Morrison.

2. Write in the principal parts of each of the following verbs.

	Present	Present perfect	Past perfect	Future perfect
a.	know	_____	_____	_____
b.	want	_____	_____	_____
c.	catch	_____	_____	_____

3. Identify the underlined verb tense.

   a. Emile <u>will have lost</u> ten pounds by spring.
   b. Susie, determined to see the world, <u>went</u> to Alaska.
   c. I <u>had left</u> before Yassine arrived.
   d. Lillie, a master gardener, <u>will plant</u> beans next year.

4. Using the verb in parentheses, supply the appropriate verb tense for the following sentences.

   a. Connor and Tess _____ five years this November. (marry)
   b. Josh _____ to New Orleans last February. (go)
   c. Mother _____ when she sees what Erik has done. (proud)
   d. We are grateful for the customers who _____us this year. (support)

5. Note if the following underlined words are functioning as *action* or *linking* verbs.

   a. David <u>called</u> us from the hospital.
   b. He <u>stopped</u> by the bicycle shop on the way home.
   c. Peggy <u>felt</u> calm despite the pressure of the match.

Answers

1. a. passive; **b.** active; **c.** passive

2. a. have known/has known, had known, will have known
b. have wanted/has wanted, had wanted, will have wanted
c. have caught/has caught, had caught, will have caught

3. a. future perfect; **b.** past; **c.** past perfect; **d.** future

4. a. will have been married; **b.** went; **c.** will be proud;
d. have supported

5. a. action; **b.** action; **c.** linking

Chapter 3

PRONOUN: WORD USED IN PLACE OF A NOUN

Chapter Check-In

❑ Identify pronouns

❑ Know when to use subjective or objective case

❑ Make pronoun references clear

❑ Ensure pronoun agreement

❑ Avoid sexist pronouns

A pronoun is a part of speech that can be used to replace a noun. There are many different kinds of pronouns: personal, reflexive, demonstrative, relative, interrogative, and indefinite.

Case refers to the way pronouns are used in a sentence, and this can be subjective, objective, or possessive. Choosing between the subjective and objective case can be confusing; for example, the choice between *who* or *whom*. Pronouns must clearly refer to their antecedents and the nouns they represent; they must also agree with their antecedents in number and gender. If you can use pronouns skillfully, your writing will be clearer.

Pronouns

A **pronoun** allows flexibility in writing because it is a word that stands for a noun. Without pronouns, writing and speech would sound unnatural and boring. Compare the following two sentences.

> Charlie left *Charlie's* house, taking *Charlie's* dog with *Charlie.*
>
> Charlie left *his* house, taking *his* dog with *him.*

The second sentence is much better.

Dividing pronouns into groups based on what they do shows how many purposes they serve.

Personal pronouns

Personal pronouns (*I, me, he, she, it,* etc.) stand for one or more persons or things, and differ in form depending on their case; that is, how they are used in a phrase, clause, or sentence. For example, when acting as a subject, the first-person singular pronoun is *I*. When acting as an object, the correct pronoun is *me*.

Reflexive (intensive) pronouns

Reflexive or **intensive pronouns** combine some of the personal pronouns with *-self* or *-selves* (*myself, himself, themselves,* etc.). Reflexive pronouns are used to reflect nouns or pronouns, as in *He hurt himself;* or to emphasize, as in *I myself don't believe it.* Although people often use reflexive pronouns as subjects and objects in speech, don't do this in your writing.

> Tom and *I* don't like it.
> NOT Tom and *myself* don't like it.

> Rob doesn't like Luke or *me*.
> NOT Rob doesn't like Luke or *myself*.

Demonstrative pronouns

Demonstrative pronouns (*this, that, these, those*) point out what you are talking about.

> *These* are the most economical, but *this* is the one we want.

When they stand alone in place of nouns, these words are pronouns. But when they precede nouns, they are adjectives: *this car, that word, these shoes.*

Relative pronouns

Relative pronouns (*who, whom, which, that*) introduce clauses that describe nouns or pronouns.

> The professor *who wrote the textbook* is teaching the class.
> The storm *that caused the power outage* has moved east.

Relative clauses are discussed in detail in Chapter 6, "Phrases, Clauses, and Sentences."

The trend is toward using *that* and *which* interchangeably, although many teachers and editors prefer to maintain a distinction. Use *that* when the clause that follows it is *restrictive:* when it provides information necessary to define your subject. Use *which* when the clause that follows it is *non-restrictive:* when it adds information that isn't necessary to define your subject. For a complete explanation of restrictive and nonrestrictive clauses, see Chapter 9, "Commas, Semicolons, and Colons."

> The car *that hit her* was green.
> NOT The car *which hit her* was green.

The relative clause *that hit her* restricts or limits the subject, car. The information in the clause is necessary to the main statement.

> The car, *which I bought a week ago,* gets good mileage.
> NOT The car, *that I bought a week ago,* gets good mileage.

The clause *which I bought a week ago* adds information about the subject that isn't necessary to our understanding of the main statement that the car gets good mileage.

Use commas around a *which* clause but not with a *that* clause. See Chapter 9 for commas with restrictive and nonrestrictive clauses.

Interrogative pronouns

Interrogative pronouns (*who, whom, whose, which, what*) introduce questions.

> *Which* is the best one to choose?
> *What* is your destination?
> *Who* asked the question?

Indefinite pronouns

Indefinite pronouns don't specify the persons or things they refer to. The most frequently used indefinite pronouns are *all, any, anybody, anyone, both, each, either, everybody, everyone, few, many, neither, nobody, none, no one, one, several, some, somebody,* and *someone.* Like other pronouns, indefinite pronouns stand in for nouns, even if those nouns aren't specified.

> *Many* are called but *few* are chosen.
> *Nobody* likes a tattletale.

Pronoun Case

Case refers to the way a noun or pronoun is used in a sentence. When it is the subject of a verb, it is in the **subjective case** (also called the nominative case). When it is the object of a verb or a preposition, it is in the **objective case.** When it possesses something, it is in the **possessive case.**

With nouns, the subjective and objective cases aren't a problem because nouns keep the same form whether they are subjects or objects.

The *frog* ate the *bee.* The *bee* stung the *frog.*

Some pronouns, however, take different forms depending on whether they are subjects or objects. These pronouns are listed in Table 3-1.

Table 3-1   Subjective and Objective Pronouns

Subjective Case	Objective Case
I	me
he	him
she	her
we	us
they	them
who, whoever	whom, whomever

In the sentence *Tension existed between Franklin and Winston,* there is no confusion about what case to use for *Franklin* or *Winston.* But what about in the following sentence?

Tension existed between Franklin and *him.*

Is *him* right? Or should it be *he?* (The pronoun is the object of the preposition *between,* so *him* is correct.)

Subjective Case of Pronouns

Pronouns are also used as subjects of verbs. Use the subjective case of pronouns when the pronoun is the subject of a verb.

I drive to work.

He enjoys dancing.

We bought the lodge.

They are fighting over the property line.

The player *who won* the game was the guest of honor.

Compound subjects

When there are **compound subjects**—that is, more than one actor—don't be confused. Pronouns should still be in the subjective case.

Eileen and he (not *Eileen and him*) enjoy dancing.

The Harrisons and they (not *The Harrisons and them*) are fighting over the property line.

To keep from making pronoun case errors in sentences with compound subjects, drop the subject that is a noun and read the sentence with the pronoun alone. You would never say *Him enjoy dancing* or *Them are fighting over the property line.* When you apply this test, you'll see that the subjective forms *he* and *they* are correct.

Pronouns following "to be"

You should also use the subjective case of pronouns after forms of the verb *to be*.

It *is I* who chose the location.

The man who called the police *was he*.

The real criminals *are we* ourselves.

The winners *were they* and the Rudermans.

The man who phoned *was who?*

The word after a form of *to be* is called a **complement.** It is also sometimes called a *predicate nominative* or *predicate adjective.*

Unlike words following action verbs, the complement of a linking verb is not an object, a receiver of action. Instead, the complement identifies or refers to the subject. Compare the following two sentences.

The president *saw Mr. Komino.*

The president *was Mr. Komino.*

In the first sentence, *Mr. Komino* is an object that receives the president's action of seeing. If a pronoun were to be substituted for *Mr. Komino,* the pronoun would be in the objective case: *him.* But in the second sentence,

Mr. Komino isn't receiving any action. *Mr. Komino* identifies the subject: the president. The correct pronoun to substitute for *Mr. Komino* in this sentence would be *he.*

Pronoun complements can cause case problems. As the rule says, the subjective form of a pronoun is correct after *to be,* but sometimes it sounds unnatural or too formal.

> It is *I.*
> I am *she.*

> The person I chose was *he.*
> The winners were *they.*

The best way to handle awkward-sounding constructions is to look for a better way to say the same thing. For example:

> They were the winners.
> OR They won. (better)

> He was the person I chose.
> OR I chose him. (better)

In informal speech and writing, modern usage allows *It is me* or *It's me.* In formal writing, either stay with the established rule or rewrite the sentence to avoid correct but awkward wording.

Objective Case of Pronouns

When a pronoun is the object of the verb or preposition, it is in the objective case. (See Chapter 2, "Verb: Word or Phrase Expressing Action or State of Being," for direct and indirect objects; and Table 3-1 earlier in this chapter.)

Pronouns as objects of verbs

Use the objective case of pronouns when the pronoun is a direct or indirect object of a verb.

> Sergio *nominated me* for secretary. (direct object of *nominated*)
> The news *hit them* hard. (direct object of *hit*)
> Jennifer *gave him* the house and car. (indirect object of *gave*)
> Chang *told us* and *them* the same incredible story. (indirect object of *told*)

Pronouns as objects of prepositions

Use the objective case of pronouns when the pronoun is an object of a preposition. (Prepositions are discussed in detail in Chapter 5, "Connecting Words and Phrases: Prepositions, Conjunctions, and Interjections.")

> The man pulled a blanket *over* the children and *us*. (Object of the preposition *over*)
>
> The man *for whom* they waited never arrived. (They waited *for whom*: object of the preposition *for*)

Pronoun over-refinement

Choosing *between you and me* (correct) and *between you and I* (incorrect) should be easy, but some people think the subjective case is more correct—that *I* is superior to *me*. Don't be influenced by a misguided idea of refinement. The phrases *for you and I* and *between you and I* are common mistakes that are probably due to over-refinement. The pronouns in these phrases are objects of prepositions and should be in the objective case. Therefore, *for you and me* and *between you and me* are correct.

Compound objects

Watch out for pronoun case when you have a compound object. Remember that when an object is more than one person, it is still an object. Pronouns should be in the objective case.

> The ceremony will be given for *Tucker, Martinez, and me*. (NOT *for Tucker, Martinez, and I*)
>
> *Without Kate and me* (NOT *Without Kate and I*), the book wouldn't have been published.
>
> The dean *nominated Nelson and me* (NOT *Nelson and I*) to serve on the committee.

You can test for pronoun cases in such situations by reading the sentences with the pronoun object alone: *The ceremony will be given for I. Without I, the book wouldn't have been published. The dean nominated I to serve on the committee.* The errors are clear. *Me* is the right form of the pronoun in these three sentences.

Pronouns as subjects of infinitives

When a pronoun is the subject of an infinitive (the basic verb with *to: to swim, to drive*, etc.), use the objective case for the pronoun. Your ear will tell you the objective case (not the subjective case) is correct.

He wanted *her to drive* the car.

NOT He wanted *she to drive* the car.

Brad asked *them to leave* early.

NOT Brad asked *they to leave* early.

Choosing Between Subjective Case and Objective Case

Choosing between the subjective case and objective case is sometimes complicated by appositives, and the *as* or *than* construction. The confusion over the choice of *who* or *whom* is a good example of this problem.

Pronoun case with appositives

An **appositive** is a word or group of words that restates or identifies the noun or pronoun it is next to: My sister *Heather;* John, *the gardener;* our friend *Carlos;* We, *the people.* The presence of an appositive doesn't change the rule for pronoun case; that is, use the subjective case for subjects and the objective case for objects.

> The decision to close the pool was a setback *for us swimmers.* (NOT *for we swimmers*)

The best way to make sure you have chosen the correct pronoun case is to read the sentence without the appositive: *The decision to close the pool was a setback for we.* You can see that *us* is the right pronoun to use.

Choosing the right pronoun case after *as* or *than* can be difficult.

> You admire Professor Morrow more *than I.*
>
> You admire Professor Morrow more *than me.*

Depending on the meaning, either choice could be correct. If the writer means *You admire Professor Morrow more than I (admire Professor Morrow),* then the first sentence is correct. If the writer means *You admire Professor Morrow more than (you admire) me,* then the second sentence is correct.

The key to choosing the right pronoun case is to mentally supply the missing part of the clause.

> Did you work as hard *as they?* (*worked*)
>
> I like Ed better *than he.* (*likes* Ed)

I like Ed better than him. (*than I like him*)

They are smarter *than we.* (*are*)

If a sentence sounds awkward to you—for example, *They are smarter than we*—you can avoid the problem by supplying the missing word: *They are smarter than we are.*

Who, whom, whoever, whomever

These pronouns cause so much confusion that they are being treated separately, even though the rules about case are the same as those for *I, he, she, we,* and *they.*

As a **subject,** choose *who* or *whoever. Who/whoever* must be followed by a verb because it is the subject.

She was the player *who won* the game. (*who* is the subject of *won*)

Whoever wants the paper can have it. (*Whoever* is the subject of *wants*)

As an **object,** choose *whom* or *whomever. Whom/whomever* is not followed by a verb because it is an object.

He was a person *around whom* controversy swirled. (*whom* is the object of the preposition *around*)

Whomever will you invite? (*You will invite whomever:* direct object of *invite*). In casual conversation and informal writing, *whom* is used infrequently. At the beginning of questions, for example, *who* is often substituted for *whom,* even when *whom* is grammatically correct, as in the following informal sentences.

Who will you marry? (You will marry *whom.*)

Who did he ask? (He did ask *whom.*)

Maybe *whom* will disappear from the language someday. Does this mean you should ignore it? No, it is still best to correctly distinguish between *who* and *whom.*

Possessive Case of Pronouns

The possessive case of nouns is formed with an apostrophe: *Keesha's* costume, *the wolf's fangs* (see Chapter 1, "Noun: Person, Place, Thing, Idea, or Activity"). But personal pronouns and the relative pronoun *who* change form to show possession.

My house is bigger than *your house.*

His anger evaporated in the face of *her explanation.*

The bulldog bared *its teeth* at us.

Our decision affected *their plans.*

The economist, *whose book* had received good reviews, agreed to speak.

Your plans are more definite than *ours.*

Be careful not to confuse possessive pronouns and nouns with contractions. Possessive pronouns do *not* have apostrophes. You have to distinguish between *its/it's* and *whose/who's*. The possessive of *it* is *its,* not *it's;* the possessive of *who* is *whose,* not *who's*. *It's* and *who's* are contractions (*it's = it + is; who's = who + is*).

The cat lost *its* whiskers. (NOT *it's* whiskers)

It's (*It is*) Friday!

Whose backpack is this?

Who's (*Who is*) the author of the book?

Possessive Pronouns with Gerunds

Use a possessive pronoun with a gerund, the verb form that functions as a noun (see Chapter 1). This rule is broken frequently, with many writers using the objective case rather than the possessive case.

I didn't like *his going* (NOT *him going*) to New York without me.

Their smiling (NOT *Them smiling*) irritated her.

Please forgive *our intruding.* (NOT *us intruding*)

Pronoun Reference

Pronouns must always refer clearly to the noun they represent (antecedent). If you understand how pronouns relate to nouns, you can avoid confusion in your writing.

Finding the antecedent

Remember that pronouns stand in for nouns. An **antecedent** is the noun—or group of words acting as a noun—that a pronoun refers to. Notice the antecedents in the following example.

Kelly lifted *Mickey* into the air and then set *him* down.

The *debt* plagued *John and Sandy. It* ruined any chance *they* had for a peaceful relationship.

Neither of these examples would make a reader wonder who or what is being talked about. *Him* in the first example is *Mickey, It* and *they* in the second example refer to *debt* and *John and Sandy,* respectively.

Unclear antecedents

In the following sentences, locate the antecedents of the pronouns.

The counselor was speaking to Dave, and *he* looked unhappy.

Who looked unhappy in this sentence—the counselor or Dave? The reader can't tell. In the following sentence, did the janitors clean the girls or the locker rooms?

After the girls left the locker *rooms*, the janitors cleaned *them*.

In the second example, your common sense tells you the janitors cleaned the locker rooms and didn't clean the girls. Sometimes you can count on context or common sense to help figure out which pronoun goes with which antecedent, but you shouldn't have to. What about in the first sentence? No clue exists as to whether the counselor or Dave looked unhappy. These are examples of ambiguous pronoun references, which will confuse and frustrate readers.

You can solve the problem in various ways, including changing the sentence structure or eliminating the pronoun, as in the following sentences.

The counselor was speaking to Dave, who looked unhappy.

After the girls left, the janitors cleaned the locker rooms.

Read your sentences carefully to make sure that all pronoun references are clear.

Indefinite antecedents

More subtle errors occur when you use a pronoun reference that is too general or indefinite or one that only you know.

I told Uncle Richard, Aunt Gretchen, and then Dad, *which* infuriated Gary.

Did telling all three people infuriate Gary, or was it only telling Dad? Rewrite the sentence to make your meaning clear to the reader.

> First I told Uncle Richard and Aunt Gretchen. Then I told Dad, which infuriated Gary.
>
> OR My telling Uncle Richard, Aunt Gretchen, and then Dad infuriated Gary.

In the following sentence, no antecedent exists for *them*. The writer is thinking "bagels" but not specifying them. *Bagel shop* is not a correct antecedent for *them*. To solve the problem, restate the noun: substitute *bagels* for *them*.

> Although Mark likes working at the bagel shop, he never eats *them* himself.

In the next sentence, the antecedent for *It* is vague, leaving the reader confused. Was it only the sky that filled the observer with hope and joy? Try substituting *The scene* for *It*.

> The hills were lush green, the trees in full bloom, the sky a brilliant blue. *It* filled me with hope and joy.

What is the exact antecedent for *This* in the following sentence?

> The paper was too long, too general, and too filled with pretentious language. *This* meant Joe had to rewrite it.

A possible rewrite might be as follows.

> The paper was too long, too general, and too filled with pretentious language. *These problems* meant that Joe had to rewrite it.

The vague *this* and the indefinite *it* are common in writing. *It* can occasionally be used as an indefinite indicator: *It's true. It is raining. It is a ten-minute drive to the school.* But don't overuse this construction. For vivid writing and clear communication, make sure your pronouns have clear antecedents.

Pronoun Agreement

A pronoun must agree with its antecedent in **number** (singular or plural) and **gender** (masculine or feminine).

In this sentence, *Galen* is the antecedent of *his, he'd,* and *his.*

> *Galen,* after saying goodbye to *his* family, discovered *he'd* lost *his* wallet.

In the following sentence, *Garcias* is the antecedent of *they,* even though it follows the pronoun.

> Until *they* buy the house, the *Garcias* are staying in a hotel.

Look at the next example. Here, *Mark and Mancini* is a compound antecedent, which requires the plural pronoun *their.*

> *Mark and Mancini* took *their* cue from the senator.

Agreement problems with indefinite pronouns

Indefinite pronouns cause many agreement problems. Some pronouns (*several, few, both,* and *many*) are clearly plural and take plural verbs and plural pronouns.

> *Several are* expected to give up *their* rooms.
> *Both brothers told their* parents the truth.

Some pronouns may "feel" plural, but are actually singular and take singular verbs and pronouns: *each, either, neither, everyone, everybody, no one, nobody, anyone, anybody, someone,* and *somebody.*

> *Each is* responsible for *his or her* (not *their*) own ticket.
> *Everyone wants* to get *his or her* (not *their*) name in the paper.

When the use of a singular form would lead to a statement that doesn't make sense, you should use a plural form. For example, in the sentence *Everyone left the lecture because he thought it was boring, they* would be a better choice than *he* for the pronoun. However, the general rule is to use singular forms of verbs and pronouns with these indefinite pronouns.

Some indefinite pronouns (*none, any, some, all, most*) fall into an "either/ or" category, taking singular or plural verbs and pronouns, depending on the intended meaning. Sometimes the distinction is subtle.

> *None* of the men *was* hurt. (*not one* = singular)
> *None* of the men *were* hurt. (*no men* = plural)

> *Some is* better than none. (*some* = a quantity = singular)
> *Some were* delicious. (*some* = a number of things = plural)

All is well. (*all* = the sum of all things = singular)

All are well. (*all* = a number of people = plural)

If a plural meaning is not clear from the context, use singular verbs and pronouns.

Pronouns with collective nouns

Collective nouns can require *either* singular or plural verbs and singular or plural pronouns, depending on meaning.

> The *team* plays according to *its* schedule. (emphasizes the unit = singular)

> The *team* couldn't agree on *their* goals. (emphasizes individuals = plural)

If you are uncertain, choose a singular verb and a singular pronoun, or reword the sentence to make it clearly plural.

> The team *members* couldn't agree on *their* goals.

Sexism in Pronouns: He or She?

When the gender of a pronoun antecedent is unknown, or when the antecedent represents both genders, which third-person singular pronoun should you *use—he* or *she?* Traditionally, *he* has been the automatic choice.

> The diplomatic *person* keeps *his* opinion to *himself.*

> The *reader himself* will decide whether *he* wants to accept Smith's premise.

Many people have objected to this one-sided view. But remedying this problem isn't easy, and usage experts don't agree on one solution for eliminating gender bias in pronouns. Here are some ways of handling the problem:

- When possible, rewrite sentences using third-person plural forms.

    > Diplomatic *people* keep *their* opinions to *themselves.*

- Use *he or she.*

    > The *reader* will decide whether *he or she* wishes to accept Smith's premise.

■ Use *he/she* or *s/he*.

> The *reader* will decide whether *he/she* (or *s/he*) wishes to accept Smith's premise.

■ Continue to use *he* throughout a piece of writing.

■ Use *she* instead of *he* throughout a piece of writing.

■ Use *their* even when the antecedent is singular.

> A *ticket holder* must check *their* number.

This book recommends using third-person plural whenever possible and *he or she* when the plural form is awkward or inappropriate. However, constant repetition of *he or she* slows the flow of a sentence, and you risk annoying your reader if you use the phrase too often. If you are writing for a class, you should check with the instructor about style preference on this issue.

The solutions aren't ideal, but they are less likely to offend than choosing either *he* or *she* exclusively and less confusing than alternating between them. These solutions also prevent the grammatical blunder of using a plural pronoun with a singular antecedent (the last choice shown above). Finally, *he or she* or the more bureaucratic-sounding *he/she* is preferable to the unpronounceable *s/he*.

Chapter Check-Out

Questions

1. Choose the correct pronoun to complete the sentences.
   a. Nicole and <u>she/her</u> bought a new car.
   b. The teacher who fell was <u>who/whom</u>?
   c. He never knew that it was <u>I/me</u> who loved him.
   d. The dolphin swam under the trainer and <u>I/me</u>.
   e. My aunt knitted sweaters for Jana and <u>she/her</u>.
   f. The president for <u>who/whom</u> we voted won.

2. In the following sentences, identify the pronoun and state whether it is demonstrative, interrogative, relative, or reflexive.
   a. Which is the better bargain?
   b. Celia braced herself for the winter blast.
   c. That was Jim's greatest achievement.
   d. The author who lived in Memphis has died.

3. Underline the pronouns in the following sentences and label them subjective, possessive, or objective.

    a. Melinda had read the book, and she anticipated the movie.

    b. The conductor saw them arrive.

    c. When the rose bloomed in November, it was lovely.

    d. That mug is mine.

Answers

1. **a.** she; **b.** who; **c.** I; **d.** me; **e.** her; **f.** whom

2. **a.** which, interrogative; **b.** herself, reflexive; **c.** That, demonstrative; **d.** who, relative

3. **a.** she, subjective; **b.** them, objective; **c.** it, subjective; **d.** mine, possessive

Chapter 4

MODIFIERS: ADJECTIVES, ADVERBS, AND COMPOUND MODIFIERS

Chapter Check-In

❑ Use adjectives and adverbs correctly

❑ Avoid problems with adjectives and adverbs

❑ Show degree with comparatives and superlatives

❑ Learn about spelling compound modifiers and words with prefixes and suffixes

Adjectives and adverbs are parts of speech commonly called modifiers. An adjective modifies (or describes) a noun or pronoun, and an adverb modifies (or describes) a verb, adjective, or another adverb.

Some adjectives and adverbs require memorizing a few rules. For example, *bad* is always used as an adjective, while *badly* is an adverb. Adjectives and adverbs can also be used to show comparative or superlative degree. By adding *-er* you can compare two people, things, or an action; or by adding *-est* you can compare more than two things.

Effective writing requires correct spelling, and compound adjectives and adverbs can cause spelling problems. Computer spell-check functions aren't foolproof! There are many rules and exceptions, so keep a dictionary handy to check spelling, and be consistent throughout your paper.

Modifiers

A **modifier** describes or limits another word or group of words. To correctly identify the modifier as an adjective or adverb, it is important to identify the word the adjective or adverb is modifying.

An **adjective** modifies a noun or pronoun. In the following sentence, *orange* is an adjective modifying the noun *curtains,* and *cool* is an adjective modifying the noun *breeze.*

> The *orange* curtains billowed in the *cool* breeze.

In the next example, *happy* is an adjective modifying the pronoun *I.* This kind of adjective, one following a linking verb, is called a predicate adjective. *Thoughtful* is an adjective modifying the noun *gesture.*

> I am *happy* because of his *thoughtful* gesture.

An **adverb** modifies a verb, adjective, or another adverb. Adverbs answer questions such as *how, how much, when, where,* and *why.* In the following sentence, *sadly* modifies the verb *smiled,* and answers the question "How did he smile?"

> He smiled *sadly.*

In the next example, *immediately* answers the question "When did they come?"

> They came *immediately.*

Here answers the question "Where did she walk?"

> She walked *here.*

Very modifies the adjective *bright:* "How bright were the curtains?"

> The orange curtains were *very* bright.

Remarkably modifies the adverb *quickly:* "How quickly did he crawl?"

> He crawled *remarkably* quickly.

When to Use Modifiers

Adjectives and adverbs don't form the core of sentences as nouns and verbs do, but they give sentences texture and precision. Without adjectives and adverbs, you wouldn't know what color the curtains were, how the man crawled, when they came, etc. Use adjectives and adverbs when they contribute directly to what you are saying. For example, in "He smiled *sadly,*" you know his smile is not like the usual happy smile. *Sadly* performs a function. On the other hand, in "He screamed *loudly,*" does the adverb add anything to the verb? No, because there is no such thing as a soft scream. Here, *loudly* is unnecessary. Avoid using adjectives and adverbs that don't add anything or that state the obvious.

Recognizing adjectives and adverbs

Adverbs often end in *-ly* (*remarkably, quickly, happily, slowly*), but not always (*here, there, fast, late, hard*). And some adjectives end in *-ly* (a *lively* child, *friendly* dog, *hilly* area). To decide whether a word is an adjective or an adverb, you should look at what part of speech the word modifies, not the word itself: Adjectives will always modify nouns and pronouns, while adverbs modify verbs, adjectives, and other adverbs. Review these examples.

In the following example, *old* and *red* are adjectives modifying the noun *barn*.

> The *old red* barn needs repairs.

In the next sentence, *very* is an adverb modifying the adjective *old*, not the noun *barn*.

> The *very* old red barn needs repairs.

Hard is an adverb modifying the verb *worked*.

> He worked *hard* all afternoon.

Here, *hard* is an adjective modifying the noun *work*.

> The *hard* work took all afternoon.

Using adjectives after linking verbs

It's natural to associate adverbs rather than adjectives with verbs because adverbs modify verbs. But with linking verbs such as *be, become, smell, taste, seem,* and *look,* use adjectives, not adverbs. (See Chapter 2, "Verb: Word or Phrase Expressing Action or State of Being," for more on linking verbs.)

> The pudding tastes *sweet.* (NOT *sweetly*)
> They were *joyful.* (NOT *joyfully*)

Notice the use of adjectives or adverbs in the following sentences, depending on whether a verb is functioning as a linking verb or an action verb.

In the following example, *grow* is an action verb meaning *to develop or increase in size,* and its modifier should be an adverb (*beautifully*).

Flowers *grow beautifully* in that climate.

Here, *grow* is a linking verb meaning *to become,* so the complement should be an adjective (*beautiful*).

Bronze *grows beautiful* as it ages.

In the next example, *smells* is a linking verb and takes an adjective, meaning the dog's odor is unpleasant.

The dog *smells bad.*

Here, *smells* is an action verb and takes an adverb modifier, meaning something is wrong with the dog's sense of smell.

The dog *smells badly.*

Problem adjectives and adverbs

Some adjectives and adverbs seem to be interchangeable but are not. You will need to remember a few rules to distinguish how they are used.

Good, well. *Good* is always an adjective: *good* bread; *good* vibrations; dinner was *good.* Don't use *good* as an adverb. Use *well,* an adverb meaning to perform capably.

She sings *well.*
NOT She sings *good.*

He listens *well.*
NOT He listens *good.*

Some confusion arises between *good* and *well* because *well* can also be used as an adjective meaning *feeling in good health.*

Mother was *well* in time to go to the play.
NOT Mother was *good* in time to go to the play.

To see the distinction between *well* used as an adjective and *good* used as an adjective, look at the following sentences, both with the linking verb *looked.*

Graham looked *good* at the party tonight. (Graham looked attractive.)
Graham looked *well* at the party tonight. (Graham looked to be in good health.)

Bad, badly. *Bad is* an adjective and *badly* is an adverb. They are often used incorrectly for each other.

> I feel *bad* about his losing the election.
>
> NOT I feel *badly* about his losing the election.

Here, *feel* is a linking verb and should be followed by an adjective, not an adverb. In the next example, *badly* is an adverb describing how the team played.

> The soccer team played *badly* in the last game.
>
> NOT The soccer team played *bad* in the last game.

In the following sentence, the adjective *bad* follows a linking verb, so the appearance of the faucet is being discussed.

> The rusty faucet looked *bad.*

When the adverb *badly* follows the action verb, it explains how seriously the faucet leaked.

> The rusty faucet leaked *badly.*

Most, almost. *Most* is an adjective meaning *the greatest in number, amount.*

> *Most* people agree that exercise is good for you.
>
> *Most* crimes go unpunished.

But *most* is an adverb when it is used to form the superlative of an adjective.

> She is the *most* intelligent woman in the group.
>
> He is the *most* appealing when he first wakes up.

Almost is always an adverb. It means *nearly. Almost* modifies the adjectives *every* and *all. Most* cannot be used to modify *every* and *all.*

> *Almost* every person agreed.
>
> NOT *Most* every person agreed.

> *Almost* all the people came.
>
> NOT *Most* all the people came.

Forming the Comparative and Superlative Degrees

As shown in Table 4-1, adjectives and adverbs change to show the **comparative degree** and **superlative degree.**

Table 4-1   Comparative and Superlative Degrees

Positive Degree	Comparative Degree	Superlative Degree
sweet (adjective)	sweeter	sweetest
sweetly (adverb)	more sweetly	most sweetly

Follow these basic rules in forming comparative and superlative with adverbs and adjectives.

Use the comparative degree when you are comparing two people, things, or actions.

> Oranges are *sweeter* than apples.
>
> Naomi sings *more sweetly* than Kate.

Use the superlative degree when you are comparing more than two. The superlative degree puts the modified word over all the others in its group.

> The strawberries are *sweeter* than the apples, but the oranges are *sweetest of* all.
>
> Of all the members of the choir, Naomi sings *most sweetly.*

Most one-syllable and some two-syllable adjectives form the comparative and superlative degrees by adding *-er* or *-est: tall, taller, tallest; smart, smarter, smartest.* The adjective's final consonant is sometimes doubled: *big, bigger, biggest; sad, sadder, saddest.* A final *-y* is changed to *-i: dry, drier, driest; happy, happier, happiest.* There are a few exceptions: *good, better, best; bad, worse, worst.* If an adjective has two or more syllables, it usually forms the comparative and superlative degrees with *more* and *most: more intelligent, most intelligent; more difficult, most difficult.*

Most adverbs form the comparative and superlative forms with *more* and *most: more slowly, most slowly; more gracefully, most gracefully; more quickly, most quickly.* There are a few exceptions: *hard, harder, hardest; fast, faster, fastest; soon, sooner, soonest.*

Be careful not to double comparative degrees: *funny, funnier* (not *more funnier*), *funniest* (not *most funniest*). Do not use the *-er* or *-est* forms with *more* or *most*. Whenever you aren't sure about how to form the comparative and superlative of a particular adjective or adverb, check a dictionary.

Adjectives and Adverbs That Should Not Be Compared

Some adjectives and adverbs should not be compared because of their meanings. One of the most frequently misused comparative adjectives is *unique,* meaning *one of a kind.* Something cannot be *more unique* or *most unique.* Something is either one of a kind or it isn't. Adjectives like this (and their adverbial forms) are absolute; in fact, the word *absolute* is an absolute adjective. Other words to watch out for are *essential,* meaning *absolutely necessary; universal,* meaning *present everywhere;* and *immortal,* meaning *living forever.* With these adjectives and adverbs, comparative degrees are meaningless.

Spelling Compound Words

Compound words can be used as nouns, verbs, adjectives, or adverbs and may be difficult to spell. They can be spelled as one word, two words, or hyphenated, depending on how the word functions and where the word appears in relationship to the word it modifies or its placement in the sentence.

When you aren't sure how to spell a compound word, consult a dictionary. If you can't find the word you're looking for, you can try applying some general principles—explained in the following paragraphs—about compound modifiers.

Compound adjectives

A **compound adjective** usually consists of two or more words that express a single idea and function as a unit by modifying a noun. Many, but not all, compound adjectives are hyphenated when they appear before nouns: *common-sense answer, cross-country trip, full-length mirror, half-baked scheme, eighth-grade students, all-day workshop, self-conscious behavior;* but *midweek meeting, secondhand truck, midcareer change, extramural event, nonviolent protest, worldwide circulation, halfhearted support.*

When a compound adjective follows a noun, the hyphen is usually omitted: The athlete was *top ranked.* The driveway was *horseshoe shaped.* The coat was *velvet trimmed.*

Using a hyphen is especially important if the compound adjective could be misunderstood by the reader. For example, a *fast-moving van* could mean a van that is moving fast or a moving van that is going fast. Your intended meaning must be clear to the reader.

Compound adverbs

Most **compound adverbs** are written as two words (*distributed all over, going full speed*). Those adverbial compounds beginning with *over* or *under* are spelled as one word (*overeagerly, underhandedly*). Adverbial compounds consisting of spelled-out fractions are hyphenated (*two-thirds completed*).

Words with Prefixes and Suffixes

With a few exceptions, words with prefixes and suffixes are spelled as one word whether they are nouns, verbs, adjectives, or adverbs, and function accordingly. Common prefixes and suffixes include *anti (antiwar), bi (bilingual), co (coauthor), counter (counterclockwise), extra (extrasensory), inter (intercollegiate), intra (intramural), mid (midlevel), multi (multitasking), neo (neorealism), non (nonbeliever), over (override), post (postwar), pre (prefabricated), pseudo (pseudoscientific), re (reexamine), semi (semiconductor), sub (substandard), trans (transatlantic), un (unexamined),* and *under (undervalued).*

Be aware that some computer spell-checkers may direct you to insert hyphens after these prefixes. Check a dictionary; if the word is not there, it is customary to use a hyphen in the following situations:

■ The second element is capitalized: *anti-British, mid-Victorian* (but *transatlantic*).

■ There might be confusion with another word: *recover* vs. *re-cover, or recreation* vs. *re-creation.*

■ The second element consists of more than one word: *non-church-attending.*

■ The prefix ends with the same letter that begins the root word: *anti-intellectual* (but *reenter, reexamine*).

Chapter Check-Out

Questions

1. Identify the following underlined words as either adjectives or adverbs.

   a. The sunset faded <u>slowly</u> over the horizon.
   b. The <u>oily</u> driveway was dangerous.
   c. Myrta's <u>golden</u> hair is lovely.
   d. The driveway was a <u>little</u> rocky.

2. Choose the correct adjective or adverb to complete the sentences.

   a. Ahmed plays the cello <u>well/good</u>.
   b. Although he said he was feeling better, Tony did not look <u>good/ well</u>.
   c. Because she missed his birthday, Judy felt <u>bad/badly</u>.
   d. <u>Most/Almost</u> all the tourists attended the musical.
   e. <u>Most/Almost</u> statistics prove otherwise.
   f. He was the <u>good/better/best</u> of the two players.
   g. That was a <u>perfect/more perfect/most perfect</u> day.

3. Provide the comparative and superlative degrees for the following adjectives and adverbs.

   a. late
   b. easy
   c. far
   d. sorrowfully

4. Which of the following underlined compound modifiers are spelled correctly?

   a. The Oceanside Restaurant is <u>worldfamous</u> for its crab dip.
   b. Their <u>longdistance</u> relationship ended this spring.
   c. Mercy Hospital specializes in <u>neonatal</u> care.
   d. She recommended a <u>cooling-off</u> period.

Answers

1. a. adverb; **b.** adjective; **c.** adjective; **d.** adverb

2. a. well; **b.** well; **c.** bad; **d.** Almost; **e.** Most; **f.** better; **g.** perfect

3. a. later, latest; **b.** easier, easiest; **c.** farther, farthest; **d.** more sorrowfully, most sorrowfully

4. a. incorrect (two words: world famous); **b.** incorrect (hyphenated: long-distance); **c.** correct; **d.** correct

Chapter 5

CONNECTING WORDS AND PHRASES: PREPOSITIONS, CONJUNCTIONS, AND INTERJECTIONS

Chapter Check-In

❏ Recognize prepositions

❏ Learn the rules for prepositions

❏ Understand conjunctions

❏ Know how to use interjections

Prepositions and conjunctions are the connecting elements in sentences. Finding the link between words is the secret to identifying prepositions. There are two guidelines about using prepositions: Avoid unnecessary prepositions, and avoid ending sentences with prepositions.

Conjunctions are parts of speech that connect words, phrases, or clauses. There are three types of conjunctions: coordinating, correlative, and subordinating. They are the keys to logically constructed sentences.

Interjections are used to express strong or sudden emotion and are usually grammatically separate from other sentences. Interjections are most effective when used sparingly.

Prepositions

A **preposition** shows the relationship between a noun or pronoun and another noun or pronoun. In the following examples, the italicized words are prepositions and the underlined words are **objects of the prepositions.**

The cat *under* the <u>fence</u>

The cat *between* the <u>fence</u> and the <u>house</u>

Everyone *except* the <u>girl</u> *in* the blue dress

A letter *about* <u>us</u>

When the object is a pronoun, remember that the pronoun should be in the objective case (see Chapter 3, "Pronoun: Word Used in Place of a Noun").

Recognizing prepositions

Prepositions aren't as obvious as nouns and verbs, so they are not always easy to recognize. Look for a word that establishes a relationship with another word. For example, in the previous phrases, how is *cat* related to *fence?* The cat is *under* the fence. How is *Everyone* related to the *girl?* The *girl* is left out of the group *Everyone.* How is *girl* related to *dress?* She is *in* it. Table 5-1 shows several words commonly used as prepositions.

Table 5-1   Words Commonly Used as Prepositions

about	before	down	off	under
above	behind	during	on	underneath
across	below	except	out	until
after	beneath	for	over	unto
against	beside	from	past	up
along	between	in	since	upon
among	beyond	into	through	with
around	by	like	to	within
at	concerning	of	toward	without

Some prepositions, called **compound prepositions,** are made up of more than one word, such as *according to, because of, in front of, instead of, in spite of,* and *next to.*

Confusing use of prepositions

The unnecessary use of prepositions is a common error. Be careful not to use a preposition where it isn't needed.

Where have you been?

NOT Where have you been *at?*

Where is Nick going?

NOT Where is Nick going *to?*

Also, don't use two prepositions when you need only one.

Don't go *near* the water.

NOT Don't go *near to* the water.

The book fell *off* the table.

NOT The book fell *off of* the table.

Ending a sentence with a preposition can cause problems. The rule that a sentence should never end with a preposition is no longer strictly enforced. Still, many writers avoid ending sentences with prepositions. If you feel ending with a preposition makes a sentence sound more natural, do so and don't worry about it.

It is a comment *to which* I will not respond.

COMPARED TO It is a comment I will not respond *to.*

I bought a pen *with which* to write.

COMPARED TO I bought a pen to write *with.*

Defining Conjunctions

Conjunctions are words that join or link elements. Like prepositions, they get a job done rather than add excitement to a sentence. But choosing the right conjunction makes the logic of your thoughts clear. For example, which of the following two sentences creates the more logical connection?

I've always disliked history class, *and* I have never failed a test.

I've always disliked history class, *but* I have never failed a test.

In the second sentence, the two clauses suggest contradictory ideas: *but* provides a more logical connection than *and.*

Coordinating conjunctions

The **coordinating conjunctions** are *and, but, for, nor, or, so,* and *yet.* These conjunctions join words, phrases, or clauses that are grammatically equal in rank.

Words: Mother <u>and</u> daughter, tea <u>and</u> toast

Phrases: We found cake crumbs all over the kitchen table <u>and</u> on the floor.

Clauses: He likes me, <u>but</u> I don't care.

Each clause (*He likes me* and *I don't care*) can stand alone as a complete sentence. The two clauses are grammatically equal.

Correlative conjunctions

Correlative conjunctions are like coordinating conjunctions except that they come in matched pairs: *either/or, neither/nor, both/and, not only/but also,* and *whether/or.*

Words: <u>Neither</u> mother <u>nor</u> daughter

Phrases: We found cake crumbs <u>not only</u> all over the kitchen table <u>but also</u> on the floor.

Clauses: <u>Either</u> you surrender <u>or</u> we'll shoot.

See Chapter 7, "Common Sentence Errors," for tips on how to maintain parallel construction when using correlative conjunctions.

Subordinating conjunctions

Subordinating conjunctions join unequal elements. A subordinating conjunction joins a clause that can't stand alone (called a **subordinate** or **dependent clause**) to a clause that can (called an **independent clause**). Clauses are discussed in more detail in Chapter 6, "Phrases, Clauses, and Sentences."

We will discontinue research in this area *unless the results of the experiment are promising.*

The clause beginning with *unless* cannot stand alone; it is subordinate to, or dependent on, the independent clause *We will discontinue research in this area. Unless* is the subordinating conjunction that links the two clauses.

The train arrived *before we did.*

Before we did is a dependent clause; it cannot stand alone. It depends on the independent clause *The train arrived. Before* is the subordinating conjunction that links the clauses.

Table 5-2 lists words that can act as subordinating conjunctions.

Table 5-2   Words That Can Act as Subordinating Conjunctions

after	before	than	whenever
although	even if	that	where
as	if	though	wherever
as if	in order that	till	while
as long as	provided (that)	unless	
as though	since	until	
because	so (that)	when	

You may notice that some of these words were also on the list of prepositions. Remember that a word's part of speech depends on its *function,* not on the word itself. A preposition shows a relationship between words and has an object, whereas a subordinating conjunction joins a dependent clause to an independent one.

The man stood hesitantly *before* the door.

In the preceding sentence, *before* is a preposition (meaning in front of); its object is *door.* The preposition shows the relationship between the man and the door.

Before the expedition can begin, the details must be addressed.

In the sentence above, *before* is a subordinating conjunction, linking the dependent clause *Before the expedition can begin* to the independent clause *the details must be addressed.*

Using Interjections

Oh! The joy of interjections! **Interjections,** words that express a burst of emotion, are not grammatically related to other elements in a sentence.

Hey! Look out! Oh, no! Bravo! Wow!

Curses are also interjections: *Damn!*

Interjections can add a sudden, emotional tone to writing if they are used judiciously. Although no rules apply to interjections, you should limit your use of them. The emotion and power of interjections will be diluted if they are used too often. Generally, although not always, exclamation marks immediately follow interjections.

Ouch! Hurrah! Mercy! Awesome! Help!

Chapter Check-Out

Questions

1. Identify the preposition and the object of the preposition in the following sentences.
   a. Ivy grew between the bricks.
   b. Within a year, Tom will be an architect.
   c. The squirrels played beneath my window.

2. Which of the following sentences are grammatically correct uses of prepositions?
   a. Would you like to come with me?
   b. He lives near to the stream.
   c. I cannot decide between Libertarians and Democrats.
   d. I left my glasses beside of my book.
   e. He is involved into environmental activism.
   f. Be quiet and listen at the instructions.
   g. We split the reward among the three children.

3. Which type of conjunction (coordinating, subordinating, or correlative) is each underlined word or phrase?
   a. We were surprised, <u>yet</u> we all laughed.
   b. <u>Whenever</u> she whistles, her cat comes running.
   c. <u>Not only</u> was he cold, but also he was hungry.

4. Underline the interjections in the following passage:
   Morgan and Lisa were determined to surprise Stacey on her birthday. "Oh, boy! She will never guess what we have planned," exclaimed Morgan. Lisa, who seemed lost in thought, suddenly cried, "Hey! We forgot to order a cake." "Oh, no!" Morgan gasped.

Answers

1. a. between, bricks; **b.** within, year; **c.** beneath, window

2. a. correct
  b. incorrect (He lives near the stream.)
  c. correct
  d. incorrect (I left my glasses beside my book.)
  e. incorrect (He is involved in environmental activism.)
  f. incorrect (Be quiet and listen to the instructions.)
  g. correct

3. a. coordinating; **b.** subordinating; **c.** correlative

4. Oh, boy!, Hey!, Oh, no!

Chapter 6

PHRASES, CLAUSES, AND SENTENCES

Chapter Check-In

❑ Recognize phrases

❑ Identify independent and subordinate clauses

❑ Understand sentence structure

❑ Distinguish between active and passive voice

Phrases and clauses are the building blocks of sentences. Phrases are groups of words that act as a part of speech but cannot stand alone as a sentence. The words in a phrase act together so that the phrase itself functions as a single part of speech. For example, phrases can function as nouns, verbs, adjectives, or adverbs. If you understand how different types of phrases function, you can avoid misplacing them or leaving them dangling in sentences (see Chapter 7, "Common Sentence Errors").

Clauses are groups of words that have a subject and a predicate. Independent clauses express a complete thought and can stand alone as a sentence. Subordinate clauses can act as parts of speech but depend on the rest of the sentence to express a complete thought.

A sentence expresses a complete thought and contains a subject (a noun or pronoun) and a predicate (a verb or verb phrase). The four basic types of sentences—simple, compound, complex, and compound-complex—use phrases and clauses in varying degrees of complexity.

Prepositional Phrases

The most common type of phrase is the **prepositional phrase.** You'll find these phrases in sentences, clauses, and even within other phrases.

Each prepositional phrase begins with a preposition (examples: *in, of, by, from, for;* see Chapter 5, "Connecting Words and Phrases: Prepositions, Conjunctions, and Interjections") and includes a noun or pronoun that is the object of the preposition.

> *in* the room
> *of* the people
> *by* the river
> *from* the teacher
> *for* the party

The object of a preposition can have its own modifiers, which also are part of the prepositional phrase.

> in *the smoky, crowded* room
> of *the remaining few* people
> by *the rushing* river
> from *the tired and frustrated* teacher
> for *the midnight victory* party

Prepositional phrases function as either adjectives or adverbs.

> The woman *in the trench coat* pulled out her cell phone.

The prepositional phrase *in the trench coat* acts as an adjective describing the noun *woman.*

> Most of the audience dozed *during the tedious performance.*

The prepositional phrase *during the tedious performance* acts as an adverb modifying the verb *dozed.*

Phrases Containing Verbals

To understand phrases containing verbals—gerunds, infinitives, and participles—see Chapter 2, "Verb: Word or Phrase Expressing Action or State of Being." Briefly, these verbals act as nouns, adjectives, and adverbs in sentences and provide additional information.

Participial phrases

A **participial phrase** begins with a past or present participle and is followed by its objects and modifiers. Like participles alone, participial phrases are used as adjectives.

> *Breathing the fresh mountain air*, Jim realized he had found paradise.

In the preceding sentence, the present participle *breathing* introduces the participial phrase, which includes the participle's object (*air*) and its modifiers (*the, fresh, mountain*). This participial phrase acts as an adjective modifying the subject (noun) of the sentence (*Jim*).

> The soldiers, *trapped by the enemy,* threw down their weapons.

Here, the past participle *trapped* introduces the participial phrase *trapped by the enemy*. The entire phrase acts as an adjective modifying the subject of the sentence (*soldiers*). Notice the phrase-within-a-phrase here. *By the enemy* is a prepositional phrase modifying the participle *trapped*. Remember that phrases can act as modifiers in other phrases.

Gerund phrases

At first, a **gerund phrase** may look like a participial phrase because gerund phrases begin with the *-ing* form of a verb (*riding, seeing, talking,* etc.) and can have objects and modifiers. But a gerund phrase always acts as a noun in a sentence, not as an adjective.

Like other nouns, a gerund phrase can serve as the subject of a sentence, the object of a verb or preposition, or the complement of a linking verb. Unlike participial phrases, which provide additional information, gerund phrases are essential to the meaning of the sentence and cannot be removed without changing the logical meaning of the sentence.

In the following example, the gerund phrase *Riding the black stallion* functions as a noun and is the subject of the verb *terrified*. Notice that the gerund phrase is essential to the meaning of the sentence.

> *Riding the black stallion* terrified Hugh.

In the next sentence, the gerund phrase *seeing the suspect* is the direct object of the verb *reported*. Notice that the entire phrase, not just the word *suspect,* is the direct object.

> The police officer reported *seeing the suspect.*

In the following sentence, the gerund phrase *talking loudly and often* is the object of the preposition *by*.

The senator made his reputation by *talking loudly and often*.

In the final example, *Calling Uncle Robert* is a gerund phrase acting as the subject of the sentence. *Asking for trouble* is a gerund phrase acting as a complement of the linking verb *is*.

Calling Uncle Robert is *asking for trouble*.

Infinitive phrases

An **infinitive phrase** contains an infinitive (for example, *to sleep, to have spent, to consider, to throw*) and its objects and modifiers. Infinitive phrases usually function as nouns, although they can also be used as adjectives and adverbs.

In the following sentence, *To sleep all night* is an infinitive phrase functioning as a noun and is the subject of this sentence.

To sleep all night was his only wish.

In the following sentence, *To take an unpopular stand* is an infinitive phrase acting as a noun. It is the direct object of the verb *did not want*.

The representatives did not want *to take an unpopular stand*.

Next, the infinitive phrase *to spend foolishly* functions as an adjective modifying the noun *money*.

He had plenty of money *to spend foolishly*.

In the following sentence, the infinitive phrase *to clear her mind* acts as an adverb modifying the verb *drove*. It answers the question "Why did she drive?"

After the confrontation, she drove miles *to clear her mind*.

Split infinitives

Breaking up an infinitive with one or more adverbs is called **splitting an infinitive.** Splitting an infinitive isn't considered the grammatical sin it used to be, but most writers avoid splitting infinitives unless they have a reason to do so.

They taught her *to spend* money *wisely*.
NOT They taught her *to wisely spend* money.

Sometimes, not splitting an infinitive is almost impossible.

> We expect the population *to more than double* over the next twenty years.

Other times, not splitting an infinitive causes ambiguity or sounds unnatural. In these cases, don't worry about breaking the old rule; clarity and smoothness take precedence over unsplit infinitives.

In this sentence, does *further* modify *Chinese efforts* or *discuss?*

> We wanted to discuss further Chinese efforts to modernize.

Splitting the infinitive makes the sentence clearer.

> BETTER We wanted to further discuss Chinese efforts to modernize.

Splitting the infinitive makes the following sentence sound more natural.

> He planned *to take quickly* the children to another room.
>
> BETTER He planned *to quickly take* the children to another room.

Types of Clauses

Like a phrase, a **clause** is a group of related words; but unlike a phrase, a clause has a subject and verb. An **independent clause,** along with having a subject and verb, expresses a complete thought and can stand alone as a coherent sentence. In contrast, a **subordinate** or **dependent clause** does not express a complete thought and therefore is *not* a sentence. A subordinate clause standing alone is a common error known as a sentence fragment.

Independent clauses

He saw her. The Washingtons hurried home. Free speech has a price. Grammatically complete statements like these are sentences and can stand alone. When they are part of longer sentences, they are referred to as **independent** (or **main**) **clauses.**

Two or more independent clauses can be joined by using coordinating conjunctions (*and, but, for, nor, or, so,* and *yet*) or by using semicolons. The most important thing to remember is that an independent clause *can* stand alone as a complete sentence.

In the following example, the independent clause is a simple sentence.

Erica brushed her long, black hair.

Next, the coordinating conjunction *and* joins two independent clauses.

Fernando left, and Erica brushed her long, black hair.

Next, a semicolon joins two independent clauses.

Fernando left; Erica brushed her long, black hair.

All sentences must include at least one independent clause.

After she told Fernando to leave, *Erica brushed her long, black hair.*

In the previous sentence, the independent clause is preceded by a clause that can't stand alone: *After she told Fernando to leave.*

Erica brushed her long, black hair while she waited for Fernando to leave.

Here, the independent clause is followed by a clause that can't stand alone: *while she waited for Fernando to leave.*

Beginning sentences with coordinating conjunctions

Any of the coordinating conjunctions (*and, but, for, nor, or, so,* and *yet*) can be used to join an independent clause to another independent clause. Can you *begin* a sentence with one of these conjunctions?

No one knew what to do. *But* everyone agreed that something should be done.

An old rule says that you shouldn't. But beginning a sentence with a coordinating conjunction is acceptable today. (Notice the preceding sentence, for example.) Sometimes beginning a sentence this way creates exactly the effect you want. It separates the clause and yet draws attention to its relationship with the previous clause.

Subordinate clauses

A **subordinate clause** has a subject and verb but, unlike an independent clause, cannot stand by itself. It *depends* on something else in the sentence to express a complete thought, which is why it's also called a **dependent clause.** Some subordinate clauses are introduced by relative pronouns (*who, whom, that, which, what, whose*) and some by subordinating conjunctions (*although, because, if, unless, when,* etc.). Subordinate clauses function in sentences as adjectives, nouns, and adverbs.

Relative clauses

A **relative clause** begins with a relative pronoun and functions as an adjective.

In the following sentence, the relative pronoun *that* is the subject of its clause and *won the Pulitzer Prize* is the predicate. This clause couldn't stand by itself. Its role in the complete sentence is to modify *novel,* the subject of the independent clause.

> The novel *that won the Pulitzer Prize* didn't sell well when it was first published.

In the next example, *which* is the relative pronoun that begins the subordinate clause. *Celebrities* is the subject of the clause and *attended* is the verb. In the complete sentence, this clause functions as an adjective describing *ceremony.*

> The ceremony, *which several celebrities attended,* received widespread media coverage.

Note that in a relative clause, the relative pronoun is sometimes the subject of the clause, as in the following sentence, and sometimes the object, as in the next sentence.

> Arthur, *who comes to the games every week,* offered to be scorekeeper.

Who is the subject of the clause and *comes to the games every week* is the predicate. The clause modifies *Arthur.*

In the following sentence, *mothers* is the subject of the clause, *adored* is the verb, and *whom* is the direct object of *adored.* Again, the clause modifies *Arthur.*

> Arthur, *whom the team mothers adored,* was asked to be scorekeeper.

Noun clauses

A **noun clause** functions as a noun in a sentence.

> *What I want for dinner* is a hamburger. (subject of the verb *is*)
>
> The host told us *how he escaped.* (direct object of the verb *told*)

A vacation is *what I need most.* (complement of the linking verb *is*)

Give it to *whoever arrives first.* (object of the preposition *to*)

Pronoun case in subordinate clauses

Who, whom, whoever, whomever. In deciding which case of *who* you should use in a clause, remember this important rule: The case of the pronoun is governed by the role it plays in its own clause, *not* by its relation to the rest of the sentence. Choosing the right case of pronoun can be especially confusing because the pronoun may appear to have more than one function. Look at the following sentence.

They gave the money to *whoever presented the winning ticket.*

At first, you may think *whomever* is correct rather than *whoever*, on the assumption that it is the object of the preposition *to.* But in fact the entire clause, not *whoever,* is the object of the preposition. Refer to the basic rule: The case should be based on the pronoun's role within its own clause. In this clause, *whoever* is the subject of the verb *presented.*

A good way to determine the right pronoun case is to forget everything but the clause itself: *whoever presented the winning ticket* is correct; *whomever presented the winning ticket* is not.

The following two sentences show how you must focus on the clause rather than the complete sentence in choosing the right pronoun case.

We asked *whomever we saw* for a reaction to the play.

We asked *whoever called* us to call back later.

In each sentence the clause is the direct object of *asked.* But in the first sentence, *whomever* is correct because within its clause, it is the object of *saw.* In the second sentence, *whoever* is correct because it is the subject of *called.*

Adverbial clauses

Many subordinate clauses begin with subordinating conjunctions. Examples of these conjunctions are *because, unless, if, when,* and *although.* (For a more complete list of subordinating conjunctions, see Table 5-2 in Chapter 5.) What these conjunctions have in common is that they make the clauses that follow them unable to stand alone. The clauses act as adverbs, answering questions like *how, when, where, why, to what extent,* and *under what conditions.*

> *When Mauna Loa began erupting and spewing lava into the air,* we drove away as quickly as we could.

In the preceding sentence, *when* is a subordinating conjunction introducing the adverbial clause. The subject of the clause is *Mauna Loa* and the predicate is *began erupting and spewing lava into the air.* This clause is dependent because it is an incomplete thought. What *happened* when the volcano began erupting? The independent clause *we drove away as quickly as we could* completes the thought. The adverbial clause answers the question "When did we drive?"

In the following sentence, *because* introduces the adverbial clause in which *van* is the subject and *needed* the verb. This clause is an incomplete thought. What *happened* because the van needed repairs? The independent clause *The group of tourists decided to have lunch in the village* is necessary to complete the thought. Again, the subordinate clause as a whole acts as an adverb, telling why the tourists decided to have lunch in the village.

> The group of tourists decided to have lunch in the village *because the van needed repairs.*

Sentences

A **sentence** is a group of words containing a subject and a predicate and expressing a complete thought. In order for this definition to be helpful, you must be able to recognize a subject and a predicate, and understand what is meant by "a complete thought."

Subject and predicate

A sentence has a **subject** (what or whom the sentence is about) and a predicate. The **predicate** tells what the subject does or is or what is done to the subject (for example, The books *were left* outside). The **simple subject** is a noun or pronoun. The **complete subject** is this noun or pronoun and the words that modify it. The **simple predicate** is a verb or verb phrase (for example, *has walked, will have walked*). The **complete predicate** is the verb or verb phrase and the words that modify or complete it.

In the following example, *Ron* is both the simple and the complete subject of the sentence. *Shot* is the simple predicate. *Shot Guido* is the complete predicate: the verb *shot* and its direct object *Guido*. (For more about direct objects, see Chapter 2.)

> *Ron shot Guido.*

In the following example, *man* is the simple subject. *The angry man in pajamas* is the complete subject. *Stood* is the verb; *stood on the front porch* is the complete predicate.

> *The angry man in pajamas stood on the front porch.*

In the following sentence, *argument* is the simple subject modified by the adjective clause *that money is a burden. The argument that money is a burden* is the complete subject. The simple predicate is the verb *originated.* The rest of the sentence is the complete predicate.

> *The argument that money is a burden probably originated with a rich man who was trying to counter the envy of a poor man.*

In the short, first sentence, the subject and predicate are easy to identify. In the second sentence, you can pick out the simple subject and verb fairly easily, despite the modifiers. But the third sentence is longer and more complicated. As you begin to write more sophisticated sentences, the simple subject and simple predicate may seem to get lost in a web of modifying words, phrases, and clauses. To ensure that you have a complete sentence, you still should be able to identify the core noun or pronoun and the core verb or verb phrase.

Expressing a complete thought

In addition to having a subject and predicate, a sentence must be able to stand on its own. It can't depend on something else to express a complete thought. Look at the following example.

> *He jumped.*

This is a grammatically complete sentence, although it's not very interesting. It has a subject (*he*) and a verb (*jumped*). It expresses a complete thought. You know what happened. You might want to know more about the person—who he is or why he jumped, for example. You might want to know more about the jump itself—when it occurred, how high it was, and so on. But the basic action is complete: *He jumped.*

The next example is an **incomplete sentence.** It still has a subject (*he*) and a verb (*jumped*), but the word *When* keeps this group of words from being a complete thought: What *happened* when he jumped?

> *When he jumped.*

The following sentence is still an incomplete sentence. Now, you know where he jumped, but the thought is still incomplete: What *happened* when he jumped high into the air?

When he jumped high into the air.

The next example is a complete sentence again. The question "What happened when he jumped?" has been answered: *he looked as if he were flying.* Even if the phrase *high into the air* were deleted, the thought would be complete.

When he jumped high into the air, he looked as if he were flying.

Sentence types

By varying sentence types in your writing, you will be able to control the pacing and clarity of the paragraphs. Using a variety of sentence types also makes for more interesting reading.

A **simple sentence** has one independent clause and no subordinate clauses.

Old-growth forests in the United States are disappearing.

Citizens must act.

A **compound sentence** has two or more independent clauses, joined by coordinating conjunctions, and no subordinate clauses.

Old-growth forests in the United States are disappearing, and citizens must act. (two independent clauses joined by *and*)

A **complex sentence** contains one independent clause and one or more subordinate clauses.

Because old-growth forests in the United States are fast disappearing, citizens must act now. (*Because old-growth forests in the United States are fast disappearing* = subordinate clause beginning with subordinating conjunction; *citizens must act now* = independent clause)

Forests that have existed for thousands of years are in danger. (*that have existed for thousands of years* = subordinate clause beginning with relative pronoun; *Forests . . . are in danger* = independent clause)

A **compound-complex sentence** joins two or more independent clauses with one or more subordinate clauses.

Forests that have existed for thousands of years are in danger, and citizens must take action. (*Forests are in danger* and *citizens must take action* = independent clauses; *that have existed for thousands of years* = subordinate clause)

In your writing, try to vary your sentence structures by making use of all these types of sentences. Don't string together a long series of simple sentences; on the other hand, don't always write compound and complex sentences. Try beginning with a simple sentence, or try following several long compound and complex sentences with a simple one. It can have a surprisingly forceful effect. Note the last two simple sentences in this paragraph.

Because America seemed to provide limitless natural resources, we spent them freely. We mined for minerals, diverted rivers, and cut down trees, many of which had been growing for thousands of years before the first settlers arrived. Over the years, America's wilderness has given way to prosperous cities, and skyscrapers have replaced giant old trees. America has succeeded. But now we are paying the price.

Sentence structure can enhance the topic or purpose of your writing (see Chapter 15, "Revising and Editing"). For example, short sentences with action verbs can accelerate the pace of a narrative essay, but you may need to use compound and complex sentences to compare and contrast ideas in an argument paper.

Active voice vs. passive voice

Use the active voice rather than the passive voice of the verb whenever possible (see Chapter 2). Sentences structured in active voice are more energetic and more concise. Look at the following examples of weak passives. Notice how the subjects and verbs determine the action in active and passive sentences:

A speech *was given* by the delegate from Michigan, and a challenge *was issued* by him to everyone attending.

BETTER The delegate from Michigan *gave* a speech and *issued* a challenge to everyone attending.

After the town *was hit* by a tornado, a call to the Red Cross *was made* by our mayor.

BETTER After a tornado *hit* the town, our mayor *called* the Red Cross.

Chapter Check-Out

Questions

1. Identify the following underlined phrases by type: prepositional phrase, participial phrase, gerund phrase, or infinitive phrase.

    a. <u>Dreaming about mice</u> is my cat's favorite hobby.
    b. Kevin wants <u>to make</u> the world a better place.
    c. <u>Lying on his bed</u>, Richard felt better.
    d. Ted sneezed several times <u>during the concert.</u>
    e. Tucker planned <u>to read</u> that book.

2. Identify the function (adverb, adjective, or noun) of the underlined dependent clauses.

    a. <u>When Dad called from Spain</u>, Mom threw down the laundry and hurried to answer her phone.
    b. The prom, <u>which is usually held in May</u>, was delayed by the late snowstorm.
    c. <u>Whoever adjusted the driver's seat</u> must have been tall.

3. Identify which of the following are independent or dependent clauses.

    a. Sherry smiled.
    b. The French impressionist collection, with all their dramatic colors and themes.
    c. To have been loved is to have known joy and pain.

4. Underline the complete subject in the following sentences.

    a. My cousin Paul, a shy young man, was married last summer.
    b. The office will be closed on Thursday.
    c. The new general manager and the retiring treasurer will meet with the board.

5. Underline the complete predicate in the following sentences.

    a. Liz walked through the dark, quiet streets, determined not to get lost.
    b. The female bear and her cubs emerged hesitantly from their long, winter hibernation.
    c. Andrei and his three cousins visited the Grand Canyon last summer.

Answers

1. a. gerund; **b.** infinitive; **c.** participial; **d.** prepositional; **e.** infinitive

2. a. adverb; **b.** adjective; **c.** noun

3. a. independent; **b.** dependent (the verb is missing); **c.** independent

4. a. My cousin Paul, a shy young man
   b. The office
   c. The new general manager and the retiring treasurer

5. a. walked through the dark, quiet streets, determined not to get lost.
   b. emerged hesitantly from their long, winter hibernation.
   c. visited the Grand Canyon last summer.

Chapter 7

COMMON SENTENCE ERRORS

Chapter Check-In

- ❑ Avoid run-on sentences
- ❑ Identify and correct sentence fragments
- ❑ Check subject-predicate agreement
- ❑ Prevent misplaced modifiers
- ❑ Follow parallel structure

After you understand what a sentence is, you'll be able to tell what works and what doesn't work. To avoid errors like run-on sentences and fragments, you should learn to recognize how complete sentences are put together. Other errors, such as lack of subject-predicate agreement, misplaced modifiers, faulty parallelism, and style problems require careful attention to the way words function within a sentence. As a critical reviewer of your own writing, you'll be able to avoid these errors.

Run-On Sentences

One of the most common mistakes with independent clauses is joining them without correct punctuation. This error is called a **run-on sentence.** An independent clause standing alone should end in a period, question mark, or exclamation mark.

Joining independent clauses

If you want to join independent clauses, you should use a semicolon, or use a comma plus a coordinating conjunction (see Chapter 5, "Connecting Words and Phrases: Prepositions, Conjunctions, and Interjections"). Using a comma *without* a conjunction is not sufficient.

> He drove off in the *Mercedes, Erica* watched him go. (incorrect)

The previous example is a comma splice, a punctuation error that causes a run-on sentence. A comma alone cannot join independent clauses.

> He drove off in the *Mercedes. Erica* watched him go. (correct)

Here, the independent clauses are separate sentences. Each ends correctly with a period.

> He drove off in the *Mercedes; Erica* watched him go. (correct)

The two independent clauses are correctly joined with a semicolon.

> He drove off in the *Mercedes, and* Erica watched him go. (correct)

The two independent clauses are correctly joined with a coordinating conjunction (*and*) preceded by a comma.

Run-ons with conjunctive (sentence) adverbs

Watch out for another kind of run-on sentence. Some words look like coordinating conjunctions but aren't. These words *cannot* be used to join independent clauses with a comma. Remember that the only time you can join independent clauses with a comma and not be guilty of a run-on sentence is when one of the seven coordinating conjunctions (*and, but, for, nor, or, so, yet*) follows the comma.

The impostors—words that look like coordinating conjunctions but are actually adverbs—are called conjunctive adverbs or sentence adverbs. The use of a comma to join a clause beginning with one of these words is common. But no matter how widespread the practice, it still creates a run-on, and most teachers and editors won't accept it. Table 7-1 shows a few of the words to watch out for.

Table 7-1   Conjunctive Adverbs

also	moreover
besides	nevertheless
consequently	otherwise
further, furthermore	similarly
hence	then
however	therefore
indeed	thus
likewise	

Some transitional phrases pose the same problem—for example, *as a result, even so, for example, in other words,* and *on the contrary.* Remember the rule that independent clauses can be joined with a comma *only* when the comma is followed by one of the seven coordinating conjunctions.

> Scientists were convinced by the *evidence; however,* the Food and Drug Administration was slow to respond.
>
> NOT Scientists were convinced by the *evidence, however,* the Food and Drug Administration was slow to respond.

> The hurricane damaged the *arena. Nevertheless,* the game was played on schedule.
>
> NOT The hurricane damaged the *arena, nevertheless,* the game was played on schedule.

> Folic acid appears to exert a protective *effect. For example,* one study showed that it cut the rate of neural tube defects by two-thirds.
>
> NOT Folic acid appears to exert a protective *effect, for example,* one study showed that it cut the rate of neural tube defects by two-thirds.

Acceptable run-ons

Run-on sentences such as those described above are basic errors. On rare occasions, joining independent clauses with only a comma may be acceptable—for example, when the clauses are very short and have the same form, when the tone is informal and conversational, or when you feel the sentence rhythm calls for it.

Live by the sword, die by the sword.

They smiled, they touched, they kissed.

I hardly recognized her, she was so thin. (The word "because" is understood here.)

You must have a good reason for writing an intentional run-on sentence.

Sentence Fragments

Most **sentence fragments** are phrases, or subordinate clauses, or combinations of the two. Don't let the length of the sentence be your guide. A sentence can be two words (*He jumps*) and a sentence fragment can be fifty words.

Recognizing fragments

At first glance, a sentence fragment may look like a sentence because it begins with a capital letter and ends with a period. When you look more closely, you'll see that the group of words is missing one or more of the elements required to make it a sentence: a subject, a verb, and a grammatically complete thought.

> *Because the mayor wanted more coverage than a single newspaper story.* (fragment)

This example is a subordinate clause. It is missing an independent clause that would complete the thought.

> Because the mayor wanted more coverage than a single newspaper story, *we called a press conference for all media.*

When you write a sentence beginning with a subordinating conjunction, make sure that an independent clause follows the subordinate clause.

> We saw the boys standing there. *Laughing and throwing cans all over the front lawn.* (fragment)

A sentence here is followed by a fragment, a participial phrase that cannot stand alone. The problem could be solved if the period after *there* were changed to a comma.

> He pointed at Tanya. *The woman who wore the hard hat and the tool belt.* (fragment)

The pronoun *who* makes this a relative clause that can't stand alone. Collectively, all of the words in italics act as an appositive (see Chapter 3, "Pronoun: Word Used in Place of a Noun") identifying Tanya, and the appositive should be joined to the main clause with a comma.

> *The chair of the committee, whose term was dependent on his party's being in power, which was, according to the polls, unlikely to be the case after the next election.* (fragment)

This example is more complicated, but it's still a fragment, consisting of a subject and two subordinate clauses, each containing phrases. You don't need to identify all the elements in this fragment, but you should realize that a predicate for the subject of the sentence (*chair*) is missing. To make it a complete sentence, add a predicate; for example: *The chair of the committee, whose term was dependent on his party's being in power, which was, according to the polls, unlikely to be the case after the next election, insisted on bringing the motion to a vote.*

The last example is typical of the sophisticated fragments that might escape your notice. Keep your eye on the three key requirements: subject, verb, and complete thought. It's particularly important to check a complicated sentence to make sure it isn't a complicated fragment.

Acceptable fragments

A few sentence fragments are acceptable, although a teacher may prefer that you always avoid them. Experienced writers may use fragments for specific reasons.

In dialogue, fragments are appropriately conversational.

> "Where are you going?" I asked.
> *"Out for a walk."* She glowered at me.

In other situations, fragments can create a desired effect, make a point emphatically, or answer a question they've asked:

> Many of the people who drove by refused to stop and help. *But not all of them.*

> Scorsese had offered me a bit part in the movie. *The chance of a lifetime!* My girlfriend wanted me to turn it down.

> Why should you consider a two-year rather than a four-year college? *For many reasons.*

Before you consider using an intentional fragment, be sure you understand correct sentence structure, because an unintentional fragment is a glaring error. Also, be sure using a fragment is warranted. Could you achieve the same effect without it? In the second example above, a dash after *movie* would achieve the same effect that the fragment does.

> Scorsese had offered me a bit part in the movie—*the chance of a lifetime!*

Subject–Predicate (Verb) Agreement

Noun-verb agreement is discussed in Chapter 1, "Noun: Person, Place, Thing, Idea, or Activity." Which verb to choose for particular pronouns (for example, *everyone, each, anyone*) is discussed in Chapter 3. But make sure you don't have subject-verb agreement problems in a complete sentence. Distractions within a sentence can make you misidentify subject and verb, leading to an agreement problem. Remember that a verb must agree in *person and number* with its subject, regardless of other elements in a sentence.

Locating the subject of a sentence

Your first job is to locate the subject of the sentence. To do this, find the verb, the action word or the state-of-being word, and then determine who or what is being talked about. Then ask yourself, Is the subject first person (*I/we*), second person (*you*), or third person (*he, she, it/they*)? Is the subject singular or plural? When you've answered these questions, you will know which form the verb should take. Singular subjects take singular verbs, and plural subjects take plural verbs.

Subject-verb agreement with a compound subject

In sentences with more than one subject (a compound subject), the word *and* usually appears between the elements.

Use a plural verb with a compound subject.

> *Drinking* a glass of milk *and soaking* in the tub *help* me fall asleep.
>
> NOT *Drinking* a glass of milk *and soaking* in the tub *helps* me fall asleep.

> A concerned *teacher and* a vigilant *parent urge* her to take the exam.
>
> NOT A concerned *teacher and* a vigilant *parent urges* her to take the exam.

If *each* or *every* precedes a compound subject, treat the subject as singular.

> *Each dog and cat is* to be fed twice a day.
>
> *Every house and garage has* been searched.

Additive phrases

An **additive phrase** sometimes makes a sentence look as if it has a compound subject. Examples of these phrases are *accompanied by, along with, as well as, in addition to, including,* and *together with*. When you use one of these phrases, you are thinking of more than one person or thing. But grammatically these phrases aren't conjunctions like *and*. They are actually modifying the subject, rather than making it compound. Therefore, do not use a plural verb because of these modifying phrases.

> The President of the United States, *accompanied by* his advisors, *was* en route to Europe.
>
> NOT The President of the United States, *accompanied by* his advisors, *were* en route to Europe.

> The *instructor, along with* the class, *is* angry about the room change.
>
> NOT The *instructor, along with* the class, *are* angry about the room change.

Phrases and clauses between subject and verb

Watch out for phrases and clauses that come between the subject and predicate in a sentence. To make sure you have the right person and number for the verb, mentally eliminate intervening phrases and clauses.

> The *speech* that provoked the demonstration and caused the closing of the university *was filled* with inaccuracies.
>
> NOT The *speech* that provoked the demonstration and caused the closing of the university *were filled* with inaccuracies.

Find the verb (*was/were filled*) and ask yourself, "What was filled with inaccuracies?" This question will help you locate the subject (*speech*). When you eliminate the intervening clauses, you will find the simple subject and predicate, which in this case is *speech was filled*.

Subject following verb

Although the standard word order in an English sentence is subject-verb-object, exceptions are common.

Don't count on word order to help you identify the subject.

> Off in the corner, out of plain sight, *sits* the famous *artist*. (the subject "artist" follows the verb "sits.")

If you decide to put a subject after a verb, be sure to check agreement.

> In the doorway *wait the head of the mob and two of his thugs.*
>
> NOT In the doorway *waits the head of the mob and two of his thugs.*

Because the subject is compound, you need the plural form of the verb.

In the sentence construction *there is* or *there are,* the word *there* is never the subject. These sentence constructions tend to be passive and vague, so it's best to limit them (see Chapter 11, "Idioms, Clichés, Jargon, Slang, Euphemisms, and Wordiness"). If you do use a *there is* or a *there are,* remember that your subject will follow the predicate. Choose *there is* if the subject is singular, and *there are* if the subject is plural.

> *There are millions* of people who would rather be poor than ask for government help.
>
> NOT *There is* (or *There's*) millions of people who would rather be poor than ask for government help.

A clearer sentence construction would be *Millions of people would rather be poor than ask for government help.*

Subject-verb agreement

The conjunctions *or, either . . . or,* and *neither . . . nor* ask you to choose between things rather than add things. If both elements are singular, use a singular verb. If both elements are plural, use a plural verb. If one element is singular and one is plural, choose the verb that agrees with the element closest to it.

> The *director or* the *assistant director is* planning to be on location.
>
> NOT The *director or* the *assistant director are* planning to be on location.

In the previous examples, both elements are singular and therefore the verb is singular. In the following example, one element (*coach*) is singular and one (*members*) is plural. Since the plural is closer to the verb, the verb should be plural (*were*).

Either the *coach or* the *team members were* responsible for the dispute.

NOT *Either* the *coach or* the *team members was* responsible for the dispute.

It is better when using a subject with one singular subject and one plural subject to put the plural noun closest to the verb or to rewrite the sentence entirely to avoid awkwardness.

Subject-verb agreement in relative clauses

Agreement problems can occur in relative clauses using *which, that,* or *one of those who.*

The verb in a **relative clause** must agree with the relative pronoun's antecedent (the word the pronoun stands for). Always ask yourself what the relative pronoun refers to.

He decided to write *novels, which are* his favorite form.

NOT He decided to write *novels, which is* his favorite form.

Novels is the antecedent of *which,* and therefore the verb must be plural (*are*). A common mistake is to choose the verb that agrees with the complement in the relative clause (*form*). Remember that the complement is not the antecedent of the pronoun.

The construction *one of those who* causes confusion when it comes to subject-verb agreement in the relative clause. Decide whether *one* or *those* is the antecedent of *who* in choosing the right verb.

In the following sentence, the antecedent is *bosses,* and therefore the plural verb *believe* is correct.

Connie is *one of those bosses who believe* in giving their employees freedom to make decisions.

The addition of *only* makes it clear that the antecedent is *one* rather than *bosses,* and therefore the singular verb *believes* is correct.

Connie is the *only one of the bosses who believes* in giving her employees freedom to make decisions.

When you use a *one of those who* construction, look at the clause beginning with *who* and then decide what the antecedent is. In most cases you will decide on the plural form of the verb.

Dr. Wolfe is *one of those teachers who entertain* students as well as teach them.

One of those business owners who believe in putting the customer first, Jim won the loyalty of the community.

Note that while the *case of the pronoun* (*who* or *whom*) depends on the pronoun's role in its own clause (see Chapter 6, "Phrases, Clauses, and Sentences"), the *number of the verb* depends on the pronoun's antecedent.

Placement of Modifiers in a Sentence

Keep related parts of a sentence together to avoid the common mistake of a misplaced modifier. If it isn't clear in a sentence which term a modifier applies to, it is a **misplaced modifier.**

Misplaced modifiers

Any kind of modifier can be misplaced: an adjective, an adverb, or a phrase or clause acting as an adjective or adverb. If you put a modifier in a place it doesn't belong, you risk confusion, awkwardness, and even unintentional humor.

He saw *a truck in the driveway that was red and black*. (misplaced modifier)

If red and black are the colors of the truck rather than the driveway, write the sentence so that this is clear.

He saw *a red and black truck* in the driveway.

In the next sentence, it's doubtful that Anna wanted to be cremated before she died, but the placement of the adverbial phrase suggests that's just what she wanted.

Perhaps anticipating what scientists would discover, Anna Anderson, who claimed to be the missing Anastasia, requested she be cremated *before her death*. (misplaced modifier)

Rewrite the sentence to make it clear that the phrase *before her death* modifies *requested,* not *cremated.*

Perhaps anticipating what scientists would discover, Anna Anderson, who claimed to be the missing Anastasia, *requested before her death* that she be cremated.

In the following sentence, the placement of the modifier *by Friday* leaves us with a question: Did we know by Friday, or would we call for a strike by Friday?

> We knew *by Friday* we would call for a strike. (unclear modifier)

To avoid any possible confusion, add *that*.

> *We knew that by Friday we would call for a strike.*
>
> OR *We knew by Friday that we would call for a strike.* (depending on the intended meaning)

In these examples, the suggested rewritten versions are not the only possible ways to correct the problem. Revise your own sentences when you find confusing modifiers. You may not only correct the problem but improve the sentence by making it more concise or changing its emphasis.

Note that the placement of even a simple modifier can change the meaning of a sentence, as in the following example.

> *Not all* the home-team players were available.
>
> All the home-team players were *not available*.

Misplaced participial phrases

Among the most common misplaced modifiers are **participial phrases.** Writers often overlook whether the subject of the participial phrase is clear to the reader.

> *Advancing across the desolate plains, the hot sun burned the pioneers.* (misplaced modifier)

The pioneers are advancing across the plains, not the sun. Make this clear.

> *Advancing across the desolate plains, the pioneers were burned by the hot sun.*
>
> OR *The hot sun burned the pioneers as they advanced across the desolate plains.* (if you want to avoid the passive voice)

No matter how you decide to rewrite the sentence, make sure the modifier is modifying the right word.

In the following example, the placement of *on the hillside* between *buildings* and the participial phrase *constructed of highly flammable materials* doesn't cause serious confusion. We probably realize that it is the buildings that are constructed of highly flammable materials, not the hillside.

> *The buildings on the hillside constructed of highly flammable materials* were destroyed first. (misplaced modifier)

But you can improve the sentence by placing the modifier next to the word it modifies.

> *On the hillside, the buildings constructed of highly flammable materials were destroyed first.*

In the next example, the question is: In his glass case, was the collector preserving the ancient woman or only her teeth?

> The *teeth of the ancient woman preserved in a glass case* were the pride of his collection. (unclear modifier)

If the answer is her teeth, then rewrite the sentence to better place the participial phrase *preserved in a glass case.*

> The ancient woman's *teeth, preserved in a glass case,* were the pride of his collection.

> OR *Preserved in a glass case, the teeth* of the ancient woman were the pride of his collection.

Dangling modifiers

Dangling modifiers are similar to misplaced modifiers except that the modifier isn't just separated from the word it modifies; it is *missing* the word it modifies. The writer has the term being modified in mind—but not on paper.

> *Having already eaten dinner,* the idea of a cheeseburger was unappealing. (dangling modifier)

The dangling participle is the most notorious of the dangling modifiers. In this example, the participial phrase *Having already eaten dinner* has nothing to modify; it is not modifying *idea* or *cheeseburger.* One way to correct the problem is to add the missing word.

> *Having already eaten dinner,* I found the idea of a cheeseburger unappealing.

In the following example, the participial phrase *Studying the lecture notes* dangles in this sentence.

> *Studying the lecture notes,* the ecosystem structure became clear. (dangling modifier)

The ecosystem structure is not the one studying the lecture notes. Rewrite the sentence to clarify.

> *The ecosystem structure became clear when I studied the lecture notes.*

In the next sentence, the infinitive phrase *To win the election* is lacking a word to modify; it cannot modify *money.*

> *To win the election, money* is essential. (dangling modifier)

Rewrite the sentence to add an appropriate subject.

> *To win the election, a candidate needs money.*

In the following sentence, *When upset and sad* is an **elliptical clause,** meaning that a word or words have been omitted. In this clause, a subject and verb are missing; they are implied but not stated: *When (she was) upset and sad.*

> *When upset and sad, her room* was her refuge. (dangling modifier)

Elliptical clauses are acceptable, but a subject must follow one or the clause will dangle.

> *When upset and sad, she used her room as a refuge.*

Parallel Sentence Structures

Parallelism in sentences refers to matching grammatical structures. Elements in a sentence that have the same function or express similar ideas should be grammatically parallel, or grammatically matched. Parallelism is used as a rhetorical and stylistic device in literature, speeches, advertising, and popular songs.

> I sighed as a lover, I obeyed as a son—Edward Gibbon
> Reading is to the mind what exercise is to the body—Joseph Addison
> Ask not what your country can do for you; ask what you can do for your country—John F. Kennedy

Parallelism lends balance and grace to writing. It can make a sentence memorable. Even in prose not destined for greatness, parallelism is important.

Faulty parallelism

A failure to create grammatically parallel structures when they are appropriate is referred to as **faulty parallelism.** In the following examples, note the difference between correct parallel structure and faulty parallelism.

> What counts isn't *how you look* but *how you behave.*
>
> NOT What counts isn't *how you look* but *your behavior.*

> The president promised to *reform* health care, *preserve* social security, and *balance* the budget.
>
> NOT The president promised to *reform* health care, *preserve* social security, and *a balanced budget.*

Check for faulty parallelism in your own writing. Nouns should be parallel with nouns, participles with participles, gerunds with gerunds, infinitives with infinitives, clauses with clauses, and so on. Be especially vigilant in the following situations.

Parallel structure in a series

When your sentence includes a **series,** make sure you have not used different grammatical structures for the items.

> He described *skiing* in the Alps, *swimming* in the Adriatic, and *the drive* across the Sahara Desert. (faulty parallelism)
>
> He described *skiing* in the Alps, *swimming* in the Adriatic, and *driving* across the Sahara Desert. (parallel)

In the parallel version, all the elements in the series begin with gerunds: *skiing, swimming, driving.* In the nonparallel version, the final element is a noun but not a gerund.

The elements would remain parallel even if the phrases following the gerunds were changed or omitted. The length of the items in the series does not affect the parallel structure.

> He described *skiing, swimming* in the Adriatic, and *driving* across the desert. (parallel)

It doesn't matter what grammatical structure you choose for your series as long as you keep it consistent.

> Elaine liked to *have* a beer, *exchange* stories with her friends, and *watch* the men walk by. (parallel)

> Elaine liked *having* a beer, *exchanging* stories with her friends, and *watching* the men walk by. (parallel)

When you use words such as *to, a, an, his, her,* or *their* with items in a series, you can use the word with the first item, thus having it apply to all the items; or you can repeat it with each item. If you choose to repeat it, you must do so with all the items, not just some of them.

> He liked *their* courage, stamina, and style. (parallel)

> He liked *their* courage, *their* stamina, and *their* style. (parallel)

> He liked *their* courage, stamina, and *their* style. (not parallel)

> She saw *a* van, car, and bicycle collide. (parallel)

> She saw *a* van, *a* car, and *a* bicycle collide. (parallel)

> She saw *a* van, *a* car, and bicycle collide. (not parallel)

Parallel structure in comparisons and antithetical constructions

When you are comparing items in a sentence, obviously parallelism will be important. Make sure that the elements you are comparing or contrasting are grammatically parallel.

> He spoke more *of being ambassador than of being president.*
> NOT He spoke more *of his term as ambassador* than *being* president.

> *The schools in the rural area* are smaller than *the schools in the inner city.*
> NOT *The schools in the rural area* are smaller than *the inner city.*

In the second sentence, *schools* are being contrasted to the *inner city.* What the writer wants to contrast are schools in the rural area with schools in the inner city.

In **antithetical constructions,** something is true of one thing but not another. *But not* and *rather than* are used to set up these constructions. As with comparisons, both parts of an antithetical construction should be parallel.

The administration approved the student's right *to drop* the class but not *to meet* with the professor.

NOT The administration approved the student's right *to drop* the class but not *meeting* with the professor.

The committee chose *to postpone* the motion rather than *to vote* on it.

NOT The committee chose *to postpone* the motion rather than *voting* on it.

Parallel structure with correlative conjunctions

Errors in parallel structure often occur with **correlative conjunctions:** *either . . . or; neither . . . nor; both . . . and; not only . . . but also; whether . . . or.* The sentence structure following the second half of the correlative conjunction should mirror the sentence structure following the first half.

The scientists disputed <u>not only</u> *the newspaper article* <u>but also</u> *the university's official statement.* (parallel: phrase with phrase)

The scientists disputed <u>not only</u> *the newspaper article* <u>but also</u> *they disputed the university's official statement.* (faulty parallelism: phrase with clause)

<u>Either</u> *I like the job* <u>or</u> *I don't like it.* (parallel: clause with clause)

<u>Either</u> *I like the job* <u>or</u> *I don't.* (parallel: clause with clause)

<u>Either</u> *I like the job* <u>or</u> *not.* (faulty parallelism: clause with adverb)

I have <u>neither</u> *the patience* <u>nor</u> *the time to complete the assignment.* (parallel: noun phrase with noun phrase)

I have <u>neither</u> the patience to complete the assignment <u>nor</u> do I have the time complete it. (faulty parallelism: phrase with clause)

Be sure that any element you want to repeat appears *after* the first half of the correlative conjunction. Look at the position of *as* in the following examples. In the second sentence, *as* appears before *either* and is repeated after *or,* which makes the construction not parallel.

They acted *either as* individual citizens *or as* members of the committee.

NOT They acted *as either* individual citizens *or as* members of the committee.

In the following example, the last sentence, *we expected* appears *before* the first half of the correlative conjunction and should not be repeated after the second half.

> *We expected* <u>not only</u> to be late <u>but also</u> to be exhausted.

> OR *We expected to be* <u>not only</u> late <u>but also</u> exhausted. (better)

> BUT NOT *We expected* <u>not only </u>to be late <u>but also</u> *we expected* to be exhausted.

Parallel structure with verbs

When you have more than one verb in a sentence, be sure to make the verbs parallel by not shifting tenses unnecessarily (see Chapter 2). Also, don't shift from an active to a passive verb.

> Kate *prepared* the speech on the plane and *delivered* it at the conference. (parallel: both verbs are active)

> Kate *prepared* the speech on the plane, and it *was delivered* by her at the conference. (faulty parallelism: active verb followed by passive verb)

Sometimes sentences use a single verb form with two helping verbs. Look at the following example.

> Robert *has* in the past and *will* in the future *continue to support* the measure. (incorrect)

To support belongs with *will continue,* but not with *has.* If you read the sentence without *and will in the future continue*, you will see this: *Robert has in the past to support the measure.* Rewrite the sentence to include a participial form for *has.*

> Robert *has* in the past *supported,* and *will* in the future *continue to support,* the measure.

> OR Robert *has supported* the measure in the past, and he *will continue to support* it in the future.

Combining Sentences

Some writers create a series of short sentences that sound choppy and lack good connections. By varying the length and complexity of sentences, you will increase the reader's interest in your ideas.

Combining simple sentences

If you have written a series of **simple sentences,** try alternate methods of combining them to vary the pace of the paragraph.

Look at the following example.

> Old-growth forests are disappearing. Citizens should take action. For example, wood substitutes and recycled materials are becoming more available. People can ask their contractors to use these products.

These simple sentences can be combined to form compound and complex sentences that flow more smoothly.

> Old-growth forests are disappearing, and citizens should take action. For example, people can ask their contractors to use wood substitutes or recycled materials, which are becoming more available.

When you combine simple sentences, let meaning be your guide. For example, use a complex sentence if you want to make one idea subordinate to another and a compound sentence if you want to join ideas of equal weight. In the previous example, the first two clauses are of equal weight: the forests are disappearing, and people should do something about it. In the second sentence, the main idea is that people should ask their contractors to use wood substitutes and recycled materials. The subordinate point is that these products are becoming more available.

Review coordinating conjunctions and conjunctive adverbs (earlier in this chapter), and subordinating conjunctions (Chapter 5), to see the relationships you can show when combining sentences.

Combining sentences using phrases

You can combine short sentences by using phrases as well as clauses. (Review different types of phrases in Chapter 6.) Look at the following example.

> Scientists first identify the defective gene. Then they can create a screening test. Physicians can use this screening test to diagnose the condition early.
>
> BETTER After identifying the defective gene, scientists can develop a screening test to help physicians diagnose the condition early.

Notice that in the second version the participial phrase *After identifying the defective gene* and the infinitive phrase *to help physicians diagnose the condition early* turn three choppy sentences into one smooth one.

Varying Word Order in Sentences

Instead of beginning every sentence with the subject, try beginning with a modifier, an appositive, or the main verb. You can also try delaying completion of your main statement, or try interrupting sentences with parenthetical elements. Look at the following examples.

Begin with a single-word modifier.

> *Suddenly* the wind rushed into the room.
>
> INSTEAD OF The wind *suddenly* rushed into the room.

Begin with a modifying phrase or clause.

> *Unregulated and accessible to all,* the Internet is a powerful tool.
>
> INSTEAD OF The Internet, *unregulated and accessible to all,* is a powerful tool.

> *In front of an audience,* she was a star.
>
> INSTEAD OF She was a star *in front of an audience.*

> *When the manager told me what the apartment cost,* I decided living at home with Mom and Dad wasn't so bad.
>
> INSTEAD OF I decided living at home with Mom and Dad wasn't so bad *when the manager told me what the apartment cost.*

Begin with an appositive (see Chapter 3).

> *A frequently misdiagnosed condition,* iron overload can lead to serious diseases.
>
> INSTEAD OF Iron overload, *a frequently misdiagnosed condition,* can lead to serious diseases.

Put the verb before the subject.

> On the narrow trail ahead of him *stood a huge bear.*
>
> INSTEAD OF *A huge bear stood* on the narrow trail ahead of him.

Greater than the novel's shortcomings *are its strengths*.

INSTEAD OF *The novel's strengths* are greater than its shortcomings.

Delay completing your main statement.

We saw the ballot measure, so important to the students, the faculty, and everyone in the community, *lose by a one-percent margin*.

INSTEAD OF *We saw the ballot measure lose by a one-percent margin* even though it was so important to the students, the faculty, and everyone in the community.

Insert an interruption—a surprise element—in a sentence. Use parentheses or dashes.

My home town—*it's more like a village than a town*—recently acquired its first traffic light.

Never sacrifice meaning or clarity for variety, however. Any technique you use for sentence variety will be self-defeating if you use it too often in a short piece of writing.

Chapter Check-Out

Questions

1. Identify the following as comma splice, fragment, or correct.
   a. Dr. Jamal Washington, a brilliant cardiologist, invented a surgical procedure that is still used in hospitals today.
   b. Although nothing prepared Miranda for the long week waiting for her test scores.
   c. Even though Jeff knew the birds were rare, he hoped they would survive, his mother treasured them.

2. Circle the correct verb form in the sentences.
   a. Neither Bill nor Elly is/are ready for the holidays.
   b. Harold as well as Jimmy drive/drives a new truck.
   c. Jenny, distracted by the falling snow, do not/did not notice the traffic.

3. Select the answer that best corrects the following sentence:

   After running the five-mile race, it began to rain and Wesley stopped.

   a. After running the five-mile race, it began to rain, and Wesley stopped running.

   b. Wesley stopped running, being as it began to rain after the five-mile race.

   c. After the five-mile race started, it began to rain, so Wesley stopped running.

4. Select the answer that best corrects the following sentence:

   Determined to propose properly, Shawn decided to get a job that would pay more, which would allow him to invest in a new suit by providing more money, and to plan for a romantic evening.

   a. Shawn was determined to propose properly so he decided to get a job and then he could get paid more and then he invested the money in a new suit and he will plan for a romantic evening.

   b. Shawn was determined to propose properly, so he decided to get a job that would pay more, which allowed him to invest in a new suit and plans for a romantic evening.

   c. Determined to propose properly, Shawn decided to get a job that would pay more so he will invest in a new suit and plan for a romantic evening.

Answers

1. a. correct; b. fragment; c. comma splice

2. a. is; b. drives; c. did not

3. c.

4. b.

Chapter 8

PERIODS, QUESTION MARKS, AND EXCLAMATION MARKS

Chapter Check-In

❏ Understand when to use periods

❏ Avoid problems with question marks

❏ Create emphasis with exclamation marks

As you write, you use periods, question marks, or exclamation marks to end sentences. Periods are used to complete most sentences, while question marks end sentences that ask questions. Exclamation marks indicate strong emphasis or emotion either in a command, an interjection, or a strongly worded sentence. Like dashes and parentheses, exclamation marks should be used sparingly.

Uses of the Period

Use **periods** to end complete sentences that are statements, commands, requests, or mild exclamations. A few simple rules about using the period are demonstrated in the following examples.

> He spends winters in Florida and summers on Cape Cod.
>
> Please open your books to the third chapter.
>
> How odd it is to see Robert sitting in his father's place.

Don't use periods at the end of phrases or dependent clauses. If you do, you create sentence fragments.

> *When she visits cities in the East,* Tracey expects bad weather.
>
> NOT *When she visits cities in the East.* Tracey expects bad weather.

Courtesy questions

If a question is asked as a courtesy, you can use either a question mark or a period. The period makes the question more routine and general; the question mark makes it more directed and personal.

> Would you please take your seat before the *bell*.
>
> Would you please take your seat before the *bell?*

Abbreviations

Most common abbreviations end in a period: *Mr., Dr.,* A.M., *etc., Tues., Sept.* Other abbreviations are written without a period. In general, you can omit periods for abbreviations written in capital letters (*FBI, CIA, IOU, CNN*) if the abbreviation doesn't spell out another word. For example, *USA* is acceptable, but *M.A.* should include periods since it could be mistaken for a capitalization of the slang word *ma.* Most abbreviations ending in a lowercase letter should still be written with periods: *yr., mo.* Exceptions are *mph, rpm,* and metric measurement abbreviations such as *ml, cm,* and *gm.* Do not use periods with state abbreviations: *AZ, CA, NY, WY,* and so on. If you are uncertain about using periods with an abbreviation, check a dictionary or style guide.

Period with quotation marks

Always place the period inside quotation marks, whether or not it is part of the quotation.

> Katie said, "I didn't take the *money.*"
>
> Aunt Francine insisted on referring to her new puppy as "*my little tootsie wootsie.*"

In the first sentence, the period is part of the quoted sentence. In the second sentence, the phrase *my little tootsie wootsie* does not end in a period, but the period for the entire sentence is still correctly placed inside the quotation marks.

Punctuation with abbreviations

If a sentence ends with an abbreviation, use only one period.

> Twyla told her mother, "I won't be satisfied until I earn my *Ph.D.*"

Uses of the Question Mark

The role of the **question mark** is to end a question, even when one question interrupts or comes after a statement. For optional use of question marks with courtesy questions, see the beginning of this chapter.

> *Who knows?*
>
> I spoke to her—*don't you remember?*—and she still refused to come.
>
> No doubt Mailani thought she was doing the right thing, *but don't you agree she was wrong?*

An exception to this rule occurs when the question is followed by a phrase or clause that modifies it. Then, put the question mark at the end of the statement.

> How could the mother be so certain of the driver's identity, *considering the shock she must have felt at seeing her daughter lying in the road?*

Commas and periods with question marks

After a question mark, don't use a period or comma, even if the sentence would normally call for one. Too much punctuation can confuse the reader, as in the following examples.

> Later Kevin understood what Gretchen meant when she asked, "*Why me?*"
>
> NOT Later Kevin understood what Gretchen meant when she asked, "*Why me?*".

> "Do you want to *go?*" Patty asked.
>
> NOT "Do you want to *go?*", Patty asked.

Questions ending with an abbreviation are an exception: Was it at precisely 4 A.M.?

Question marks with quotation marks

If the material being quoted is a question, put the question mark inside the quotation marks.

> "*Do you think I'll get the job?*" Susannah asked.
>
> David looked around and asked, "*Who can speak for this man?*"

If the quotation is *not* a question, put the question mark outside the quotation marks. If the quoted material would normally end with a period, drop the period.

> *Who said,* "All that glitters is not gold"*?*
>
> NOT *Who said,* "All that glitters is not *gold.*"*?*

Problems with Question Marks

Two problem situations involving question marks are the indirect question and the sarcastic or emphatic question. These are special cases that require you to be clear about your intended meaning.

Indirect questions

When a question is being *reported* rather than directly asked, it ends with a period rather than a question mark. Compare the following sentences.

> Ethan asked, "What made the stars so brilliant tonight?" (direct question)
>
> Ethan asked what made the stars so brilliant tonight. (indirect question with the intent of a statement)

Sarcastic and emphatic question marks

Don't use a question mark inside parentheses to indicate sarcasm (as in the first example below). If you want to emphasize a sarcastic tone, consider using quotation marks and italic type (as in the second example).

> The actor said his interest in the orphans was purely altruistic (?) and that the presence of the photographers was coincidental. (Inserting a question mark in parentheses is not advisable.)
>
> The actor said his interest in the orphans was "*purely altruistic*" and that the presence of the photographers was coincidental. (This example shows the sarcastic tone more clearly.)

Be careful not to overuse quotation marks and italic type to indicate a sarcastic tone. See the warnings in Chapter 10, "Dashes, Parentheses, and Quotation Marks."

Never use more than one question mark for emphasis.

> Do you really want to risk your life skydiving?
>
> NOT Do you really want to risk your life skydiving??

The word *really* emphasizes the point, as does the use of italics.

Uses of the Exclamation Mark

Exclamation marks follow interjections (see Chapter 5, "Connecting Words and Phrases: Prepositions, Conjunctions, and Interjections") and other expressions of strong feeling. They may also be used to lend force to a command.

> *What a mess!*
>
> *The lights! The music! The dazzling costumes!* My eyes and ears couldn't get enough of the spectacle.
>
> *Sit down and shut your mouth! Now!*

An exclamation mark is particularly useful if you're writing dialogue because it shows the speaker's feeling behind a statement.

Exclamation marks with quotation marks

If the material being quoted is an exclamation, put the exclamation mark inside the quotation marks.

> "*I hate you!*" she screamed.
>
> "*Baloney!*" he said, storming out of the room.

If an exclamation includes a quotation that is not an exclamation, put the exclamation mark outside the quotation marks.

> For the last time, *stop calling me your "darling little boy"!*

Exclamation marks with commas and periods

After an exclamation mark, omit a comma or a period.

> "*You adorable thing!*" he gushed.
>
> NOT "*You adorable thing!,*" he gushed.

> *What a terrible way to end our trip!*
>
> NOT *What a terrible way to end our trip!.*

Problems with Exclamation Marks

Overuse of exclamation marks dulls their effect. Do not use more than one exclamation mark at the end of a sentence.

> The film's last scene poignantly showed that his battle had been for nothing, and he had lost her and his dream forever.

> NOT The film's last scene was so *poignant!* You knew he'd lost her forever! His dream was *dead!!*

Also, avoid using an exclamation mark in parentheses to indicate sarcasm or irony. Instead, rely on vivid language to communicate the desired meaning.

> Mom was convinced that Marie's self-confidence problem could be solved with a new dress, and she refused to discuss the issue further.

> NOT Mom thought that Marie's self-confidence problem could be solved with a new dress (*!*), and she didn't want to discuss the issue further.

Chapter Check-Out

Questions

1. Insert a question mark, exclamation mark, or period in the appropriate blank in the following sentences. If further punctuation is not needed, write NP (no punctuation) in the blank.

    a. "Hey___"___ Rebecca cried.
    b. Chip asked, "When does the bus leave___"___
    c. The candidate claimed the embezzlement was accidental___, but we knew better.
    d. Sick of winter, Susan asked when the snow would stop___

2. Insert a period, question mark, or quotation mark in the appropriate blank in the following sentences. If punctuation is not needed, write NP.

    a. "Surprise___" Mr. Farrell's class cried in unison___
    b. Amanda's birthday is Monday___—have you forgotten___
    c. Clay said, "The car will be ready today___"___

3. Note which sentences are correct or incorrect.

    a. He lied about his health. He wanted to protect her feelings.
    b. Even though she lost. Anna was a good sport.
    c. Mr. Spence told Tom, "Leave your plans with our client".
    d. He told us, "Natasha is now working on her M.A.".
    e. Evelyn called Caleb Jones, M.D.

Answers

1. a. !, NP; **b.** ?, NP; **c.** NP; **d.** period

2. a. !, period; **b.** NP, ?; **c.** period, NP

3. a. correct
    b. incorrect (Even though she lost, Anna was a good sport.)
    c. incorrect (Mr. Spence told Tom, "Leave your plans with our client.")
    d. incorrect (He told us, "Natasha is now working on her M.A.")
    e. correct

Chapter 9

COMMAS, SEMICOLONS, AND COLONS

Chapter Check-In

❑ Learn the rules for commas

❑ Use semicolons in sentences

❑ Master the use of colons

Commas indicate pauses or brief breaks between ideas in sentences. They add pacing and clarity. Many writers either neglect to use or overuse commas, which complicates their sentences, or can sometimes obscure the meaning. The rules about commas are straightforward and not difficult to learn.

Many writers are confused about when to use a semicolon and when to use a colon. The main rule for these punctuation marks is to use them sparingly. Semicolons join independent clauses and items in a series. Colons introduce a list, a quote or formal statement, a restatement, or an explanation. Once you master the rules for effective punctuation, your writing skills will improve.

Uses of the Comma

Commas are used after introductory clauses and phrases, to set off interruptions within the sentence, with nonrestrictive phrases and clauses, and between items or modifiers in a series. Commas can also join independent clauses as long as the comma is followed by a coordinating conjunction (*for, and, nor, but, or, yet, so*).

There are special situations in which commas should also be used. For example, use commas with quotations, dates, addresses, locations, and numbers with four or more digits. Commas should never be used around restrictive clauses, to separate a subject and verb, or to separate a verb and its direct object.

As you learn about commas, first, recognize that they signal a pause; second, know which rules can be bent without misleading your reader. Commas are the most frequently used internal punctuation in sentences, and people have more questions about them than about any other punctuation mark. One reason is that different editors have different opinions about when a comma is needed. You're likely to read one book in which commas abound, while in another text, they are scarce. The trend has been toward fewer commas.

Sometimes a comma is absolutely necessary to ensure the meaning of a sentence, as in the following examples.

> Because I wanted to *help, Dr. Hodges,* I pulled the car over to the side of the road.

> Because I wanted to *help Dr. Hodges,* I pulled the car over to the side of the road.

In the first sentence, the pair of commas indicates that Dr. Hodges is being addressed. In the second sentence, Dr. Hodges is the one receiving the help. Most situations, however, aren't this clear.

Joining independent clauses

Generally, when you join independent clauses with a coordinating conjunction, insert a comma before the conjunction.

> Ryan never answered these charges, *but* he was later forced to give up part of the money.

> The novel lacks fully developed characters, *and* the plot is filled with unlikely coincidences.

If the two independent clauses are short and closely related, you may use a comma or omit it, depending on whether or not you want to indicate a pause.

> It was an admirable *scheme and* it would work.

> OR It was an admirable *scheme, and* it would work.

> The night was *cold and* the sky was clear.

> NOT The night was *cold, and* the sky was clear.

When you insert a comma between independent clauses, it *must* be accompanied by one of the coordinating conjunctions. If it isn't, you create a comma splice (see Chapter 7, "Common Sentence Errors").

It had been a tumultuous year that had taken everybody by *surprise, and* it left the revolutionaries worse off than they had been before.

NOT It had been a tumultuous year that had taken everybody by *surprise, it* left the revolutionaries worse off than they had been before.

After introductory clauses

It is customary to use a comma after an **introductory adverbial clause.** (For adverbial clauses, see Chapter 6, "Phrases, Clauses, and Sentences.") With a lengthy clause, the comma is essential.

After she walked into the room, we stopped gossiping.

If you receive inappropriate material, acknowledge it by explaining to the correspondent why the material won't see print.

You may omit the comma if the subordinate clause is short and if there is no possibility for miscommunication.

When she arrived we stopped gossiping.

After I turned sixteen I was allowed to stay out until midnight.

Sometimes omitting a comma will cause confusion or amusement, as in the following example.

When we are cooking the children cannot come into the kitchen. (no)

When we are cooking, the children cannot come into the kitchen. (yes)

Remember that, unlike a clause, a phrase is a group of words without a subject and a verb (see Chapter 6).

If an **introductory phrase** is more than a few words, it's a good idea to follow it with a comma. Always use a comma if there is any possibility of misunderstanding the sentence without one.

By taking the initiative to seek out story leads, a reporter will make a good impression on the editor.

At the beginning of the visiting professor's lecture, most of the students were wide awake.

Unlike many performances of the symphony, this one was spirited and lively.

Before eating, Cameron always runs two miles on the beach.

Note that the introductory phrase in the last example, although short, would lead to a misunderstanding if the comma were omitted.

A **participial phrase** at the beginning of a sentence is *always* followed by a comma.

Smiling and shaking hands, the senator worked her way through the crowd.

Do not confuse a participial phrase with a **gerund phrase,** however (see Chapter 6). A gerund phrase that begins a sentence should *not* be followed by a comma. Compare the following two sentences.

Thinking of the consequences, she agreed not to release the memo to the press. (introductory participial phrase, modifying *she:* use a comma)

Thinking of the consequences gave her a tremendous headache. (gerund phrase, functioning as the subject of the sentence: do not use a comma)

Use of a comma after most short introductory phrases is optional.

Later that day Jack and Linda drove to the ocean.

After the main course I was too full for dessert.

The best way to decide whether to use a comma is to read the sentence aloud and see if you pause after the introductory phrase. If you pause, use a comma.

To set off interrupting elements

Some phrases, clauses, and terms interrupt the flow of a sentence and should be enclosed in commas. Examples of these interrupters are conjunctive adverbs, transitional phrases, and names in direct address.

Conjunctive adverbs and transitional phrases—*consequently, as a matter of fact, of course, therefore, on the other hand, for example, however, to tell the truth*—are usually followed by commas when they begin sentences.

For example, you shouldn't use an acid solution on soft surfaces.

Therefore, he refused to go with us.

When they interrupt a sentence, they are usually enclosed in commas.

> As the project moves along, *of course,* you will be given greater independence.
>
> One who excels at research, *for example,* might be assigned to the library.

A name or expression used in direct address is always followed by a comma, or enclosed in commas when it interrupts the sentence.

> *Fellow citizens,* I am here to ask for your support.
>
> I tell you, *Jason,* I will not be forced into this by you or anyone.
>
> Yes, *readers,* I am telling you the truth.

Other interrupters may also require commas. Check your sentence for elements outside the main flow of the sentence and enclose them in commas.

> It is too early, *I believe,* to call in the police.
>
> The historical tour, *we were led to believe,* was organized by experts.

Although dashes and parentheses can also be used to set off some kinds of interrupting elements (see Chapter 10, "Dashes, Parentheses, and Quotation Marks"), commas are better when you want to draw less attention to an interruption.

With restrictive and nonrestrictive elements

Look at the following two sentences. In the first sentence, *who arrived yesterday* is a **restrictive** clause—that is, one that restricts, limits, or defines the subject of the sentence. In the second sentence, the same clause is **nonrestrictive**—that is, it doesn't restrict or narrow the meaning but instead adds information. A restrictive element is essential to the reader's understanding; a nonrestrictive element is not.

> The women *who arrived yesterday* toured the island this afternoon.
>
> The women, *who arrived yesterday,* toured the island this afternoon.

In the first sentence, *who arrived yesterday* defines exactly which women are the subject of the sentence, separating them from all other women. In the second sentence, the information *who arrived yesterday* is additional information but is not essential to the meaning of the sentence. It does not separate the women from all other women. As the writer, you must decide which kind of information you intend.

Commas make all the difference in meaning here. Restrictive (or essential) elements should not be enclosed in commas, while nonrestrictive (or nonessential) elements should be. Review the following sentences.

> The workers *who went on strike* were replaced. (restrictive)
>
> The workers, *who went on strike,* were replaced. (nonrestrictive)

In the first sentence, only *some* workers were replaced. The absence of commas restricts the subject to only those workers who went on strike. In the second sentence, *all* the workers were replaced. The information that they went on strike is not essential; it doesn't define which workers were replaced.

In the following sentence, the phrase *who are over age sixty* is essential in limiting the subject *workers* and therefore should not be enclosed in commas. The second sentence means that all workers are over age sixty, which isn't logical.

> Workers *who are over age sixty* have difficulty finding a new job.
>
> NOT Workers, *who are over age sixty,* have difficulty finding a new job.

Whether to use commas around modifying elements is based entirely on whether the element is restrictive (essential or limiting) or nonrestrictive (additional information).

> My brother, *who is thirteen,* watches television more than he reads. (additional information)
>
> The man *who took the pictures* is being sued for invasion of privacy. (essential)
>
> Cats, *more independent than dogs,* are good pets for people who work all day. (additional information)
>
> Cats *who are fussy eaters* are a trial to their owners. (essential)
>
> My brother, *while swimming in the ocean,* saw a jellyfish. (additional information)
>
> People *swimming in the ocean* should watch for jellyfish. (essential)

With appositives

Appositives are words that restate or identify a noun or pronoun (see Chapter 3, "Pronoun: Word Used in Place of a Noun"). When appositives are nonrestrictive, they are enclosed in commas.

Kublai Khan, *grandson of Genghis,* was the first Mongol emperor of all China.

Jack Kerouac, *one of the most famous of the Beat Generation writers,* came to symbolize the era he wrote about.

Sometimes an appositive is essential because it limits the subject. It must *not* be enclosed in commas. Look at the following examples.

Shakespeare's play *Hamlet* was probably written about 1600.

NOT Shakespeare's play, *Hamlet,* was probably written about 1600.

In this example, if you enclose *Hamlet* in commas, you limit the meaning and communicate that Shakespeare wrote only one play.

Between Items in a series (serial comma)

It is considered standard practice to use commas to separate items in a series, called a **serial comma** (example: red, white, and blue). Although some editors feel that it is acceptable to omit the final comma in a series, it's clearer and easier to consistently insert the comma before the final element.

He bought a *dishwasher, microwave, refrigerator, and washer* from the outlet store.

Her play is filled with *coincidences, false anticipations, and nonresponsive dialogue.*

Omitting a final comma may create ambiguity. Since you should be consistent throughout a piece of writing, you might want to get in the habit of always using the serial comma.

The following examples show the serial comma separating a series of items.

The millionaire's estate was to be divided among his *housekeeper, the gardener, his sons, and the grandchildren.*

The recipe said to mix the *flour, sugar, eggs, and milk* together.

She warned us about the *subway, the elevators at Bloomingdale's, and the Metropolitan Museum of Art.*

The following examples do not have the serial comma and can be ambiguous in meaning.

The millionaire's estate was to be divided among his *housekeeper, the gardener, his sons and the grandchildren.*

The recipe said to mix the *flour, sugar, eggs and milk* together.

She warned us about the *subway, the elevators at Bloomingdale's and the Metropolitan Museum of Art.*

Don't use commas if *all* items in a series are joined by *and* or *or.*

He asked to see *Martha and Helen and Eileen.*

NOT He asked to see *Martha, and Helen, and Eileen.*

Between modifiers in a series

Modifiers in a series are usually separated with commas. But don't put a comma between the final modifier and the word it modifies.

It was a *dark, gloomy, forbidding* house.

NOT It was a *dark, gloomy, forbidding,* house.

All three modifiers—*dark, gloomy,* and *forbidding*—modify *house.*

Sometimes, what seems to be a modifier is actually part of the element being modified. Look at the following examples.

He is a tall, good-looking, intelligent young man.

Young man, not just *man,* is the element being modified. Therefore, don't use a comma after *intelligent.*

They bought a *beautiful, spacious summer* home.

Summer home, not just *home,* is being modified. Don't use a comma after *spacious.*

To test whether you should use a comma before the last adjective in a series, see if it makes sense to reverse the order of the adjectives. If you can reverse them without changing the meaning or eliminating sense, then use commas between them. If you can't, don't.

It was a *dark, gloomy, forbidding* house.

It was a *forbidding, dark, gloomy* house. (no change in meaning)

In the previous example the order of the adjectives *can* change; therefore, use commas between them.

They bought a *beautiful, spacious summer* home.

They bought a *summer, beautiful, spacious* home. (does not make sense)

In the second sentence, changing the order of the adjectives makes the sentence nonsensical. Therefore, you would *not* use a comma between *spacious* and *summer*.

Commas with quotation marks

Commas always go inside quotation marks, whether or not they are part of the quotation.

He called her "*the worst boss in the world,*" and he sent a series of threatening letters.

"I can't believe you ate the entire *watermelon,*" she said.

Miscellaneous uses of the comma

There are some special situations in which commas are necessary. Use commas in the following instances:

■ To present quotations, with *he said, she muttered,* etc.

He said, "Let's go."

"Wait a while," *she said,* "and I will."

■ Between items in dates and addresses (except between state and zip code)

1328 Sailor Road, Santa Paula, CA 93060

December 10, 1962

■ Between cities and counties, cities and states, and states and countries

Boise, Idaho

■ To set off items in dates and addresses within sentences

December 10, 1962, was her birthday.

He lived at 23 Park Street, Boise, Idaho, until he left for *Chiapas, Mexico.*

■ In numbers of more than four digits

50,000

293,456,678

- After salutations and closings in letters

  Dear Rachel,

  Sincerely,

- To enclose a title or degree

  Jeff Nelson, *D.D.S.,* spoke at the dinner.

Problems with Commas

One of the most common mistakes people make with commas is putting them where they absolutely don't belong.

Don't use commas around restrictive elements.

The novel *Naked Lunch* was banned from the school library.

NOT The novel, *Naked Lunch,* was banned from the school library.

Don't separate subject from verb with a comma.

The girl in the window is not my sister.

NOT *The girl in the window*, is not my sister.

Don't separate a verb and a direct object or complement with a comma.

I saw immediately the mistake I had made.

NOT I saw immediately, the mistake I had made.

When your sentence includes paired elements—for example, with correlative conjunctions—don't use a comma to separate them.

I wanted *either a trip to Europe or a new BMW.*

NOT I wanted either a trip to Europe, or a new BMW.

If you are unsure about adding a comma, check the rules. If the answer isn't there, trust your ear to tell you when a pause is important.

Uses of the Semicolon

Some writers mistakenly use semicolons to connect fragments or sentences that really should be two separate sentences. Use the **semicolon** to connect two independent clauses or a series of items.

Joining independent clauses

A semicolon is like a period. While a period keeps two independent clauses apart and turns them into separate sentences, a semicolon joins them to show a close connection. Compare these examples.

> I helped the committee all I *could*. *I* even searched the back issues of the paper to find evidence.

> I helped the committee all I *could; I* even searched the back issues of the paper to find evidence.

> I helped the committee all I *could, and I* even searched the back issues of the paper to find evidence.

All three examples are punctuated correctly. The semicolon emphasizes a close relationship between the two independent clauses that can stand alone as an independent sentence. Often, you'll find a transitional phrase following a semicolon.

> The results of the inquiry were *unclear; however,* the head of the project resigned.

> I planned the new garden to include my favorite *flowers; for example,* I like daisies, roses, and tulips.

Don't use a semicolon if there is not a close connection between clauses.

> It was time to *vote;* we were sick of the endless wrangling. (correct)

> It was time to *vote;* the secretary carried lunch in and put it on the table. (incorrect, unless the vote relates closely to serving lunch)

You may follow a semicolon that divides independent clauses with a coordinating conjunction (see Chapter 5, "Connecting Words and Phrases: Prepositions, Conjunctions, and Interjections.") In the following example, it's correct to use a comma before *but*. Also, because there are already two commas in the second clause, a semicolon better indicates the main break in the sentence.

> That night the fox appeared to *revive; but* when we woke in the morning, full of hope that we had saved it, we were saddened to find its body at the edge of the clearing.

Between items in a series

In a series, use a semicolon between items if the items are particularly long or if they contain commas.

The planning committee included David H. Takahashi, president of the Kiwanis *Club;* Leroy Carter, head of the small business owners *group;* Romana Gilbert, editor of the local *paper;* and Irma Quintero, Spanish department chairperson at the community college.

Jesse's report states that the college, plagued by financial worries, cannot fulfill these *needs;* that the community response, while positive, has not resulted in financial *donations;* and that charitable organizations, service clubs, and private donors have been overwhelmed with similar requests.

When semicolons are used in a series, the items in the series do not have to be independent clauses.

Semicolons with quotation marks

When dealing with quotation marks, *always* place semicolons *outside* quotation marks.

He asked me to be quiet and mind my *"atrocious manners";* I told him I'd speak my mind.

Mr. Miser wanted to use words like *"prohibit"* and *"forbid";* to devise strong, painful punishments for *infractions;* to publish this book of rules as soon as *possible;* and, in a bountiful gesture, to distribute it to the orphans with their gruel.

Problems with Semicolons

Except when used to separate items in a series, a semicolon *must* be followed by an independent clause or else you create a sentence fragment.

I expected to win the debate; *even if my opponent had more experience.* (sentence fragment)

I had studied the subject thoroughly; *and researched even the minor points.* (sentence fragment)

These sentences could be corrected either by changing the punctuation within the sentence or by making the second clause independent.

I expected to win the *debate, even* if my opponent had more experience. (correct)

I had studied the subject *thoroughly; I* had researched even the minor points. (correct)

Uses of the Colon

A **colon** is used to introduce a list. It can be a formal introduction using *as follows,* or less formal.

> The ceremony to honor Dr. Mills included *everything:* a moving introduction, a recitation of her achievements, a series of testimonials, and a glowing forecast of her future in the new position.
>
> The questions were *as follows:* Where did you last work? For how long? What was your job title? What were your primary achievements?

Also, use a lowercase letter after the colon unless the list is a series of complete sentences, as in the second example. Use a capital letter after a colon in the situations described below.

Introducing a quotation or formal statement

The colon is used to introduce a quotation or formal statement. An independent clause must precede the colon. Capitalize the first word of a sentence following a colon only if the text that follows is a quotation or formal statement.

> *The speaker made the following observation:* "In the future, communication between people all over the world will lead not to an enriched culture but to a homogenous one."

Introducing a restatement or explanation

A colon may be used between two independent clauses when the second clause explains or restates the first clause.

> The program was an unqualified success: *hundreds of people attended.*
>
> These shoes are the best: *they are durable, inexpensive, and stylish.*

Notice that when the colon is used in this way (like a semicolon), it may be followed by a lowercase letter.

To test whether you should use a semicolon or a colon between clauses, ask yourself whether you could logically insert the phrase *that is* after the punctuation. If you can, use a colon; if you can't, use a semicolon.

> These shoes are the best: *that is,* they are durable, inexpensive, and stylish. (correct)

A colon is appropriate in the previous example. The second clause explains the first clause. In the next sentence, the phrase *that is* doesn't work. Therefore, a semicolon is correct.

> He struggled for years; *that is,* success finally arrived. (not logical)
>
> He struggled for years; *success* finally arrived. (correct)

Colons with quotation marks

When using quotes in a sentence, *always* place colons *outside* quotation marks.

> The article was called "*The Last Word*": his definitive statement.
>
> This statement is from an article called "*Good Advice*": "Before you decide to marry a man, check out his relationship with his mother."

Miscellaneous uses of the colon

A colon is used in the following special situations:

- To separate hours and minutes when writing the time

  4:15 P.M.

  8:00 A.M.

- To separate volume and number, or volume and page number of a magazine

  Entertainment Weekly VI:4

  National Geographic 87:53-56

- To separate chapter and verse numbers for biblical passages

  Matthew 4:16

- To introduce a subtitle

  Jane Austen: A Feminist's View

- In the salutation of a business letter

  Dear Dr. Aguinaldo:

Problems with Colons

Don't use a colon to separate sentence elements that belong together, such as an action verb from its objects or a linking verb from its complements.

> The university sent *us catalogs,* maps, housing applications, and transportation information.

> NOT The university sent *us: catalogs,* maps, housing applications, and transportation information.

> The four things I want *are success* in business, a happy marriage, creative fulfillment, and peace of mind.

> NOT The four things I want *are: success* in business, a happy marriage, creative fulfillment, and peace of mind.

Chapter Check-Out

Questions

1. Place commas in the correct locations in the sentences below.

    a. Derek and Barbara who both graduated from Princeton are expecting their first baby a girl in April.

    b. My new sister-in-law Hong Anh will be flying in from Hanoi Vietnam today.

    c. Even though the weather was warm the seeds did not sprout.

    d. I read about the Mayans a fascinating culture in Mexico.

    e. As a matter of fact the loggerhead turtles are endangered.

    f. Sabitha said "Call before noon."

2. Identify whether the following sentences require a semicolon, a colon, or a comma.

    a. A good hostess must plan the menu carefully the party's success may depend on the food.

    b. The award show featured the following performers rap musicians, pop musicians, two alternative bands, and even some jazz artists.

    c. I cleaned my room thoroughly I even cleaned out the closet.

    d. He is extremely thoughtful and he never forgets my birthday.

3. Note which of the following sentences show correct or incorrect comma usage.

   a. "Don't be late," she exclaimed.
   b. The ship, *City on the Sea,* docked last night.
   c. City General Hospital, on top of the hill, is where I was born.
   d. Betty cautiously held, the antique vase.
   e. William Sheehy, our postman, was born in Ireland.

Answers

1. **a.** Derek and Barbara, who both graduated from Princeton, are expecting their first baby, a girl, in April.
   b. My new sister-in-law, Hong Anh, will be flying in from Hanoi, Vietnam today.
   c. Even though the weather was warm, the seeds did not sprout.
   d. I read about the Mayans, a fascinating culture in Mexico.
   e. As a matter of fact, loggerhead turtles are endangered.
   f. Sabitha said, "Call before noon."

2. **a.** semicolon; **b.** colon; **c.** semicolon; **d.** comma

3. **a.** correct; **b.** incorrect; **c.** correct; **d.** incorrect; **e.** correct

Chapter 10

DASHES, PARENTHESES, AND QUOTATION MARKS

Chapter Check-In

❑ Know when to use a dash

❑ Use parentheses correctly

❑ Learn the rules for quotation marks

Dashes and parentheses are interruptions within the sentence that can provide extra information. In many cases, they may be necessary and valuable additions. Brackets are used only when inserting material into parentheses or around a word or phrase of your own that is added to a quotation.

Beginning writers sometimes overuse these punctuation marks. Generally, your writing should be direct and well organized, which means you will use dashes or parentheses sparingly.

Uses of the Dash

Think of the **dash** as indicating an interruption you want to call attention to. Other punctuation marks—commas and parentheses—serve similar purposes. Commas are more neutral, and parentheses usually enclose information that is extra and incidental.

Interrupting a sentence

If you want to interrupt your sentence with a phrase or clause, consider using a dash. Or if the sentence continues after the interruption, use a pair of dashes.

She was extraordinarily tall—*the tallest woman I'd ever seen.*

She walked in—*the tallest woman I'd ever seen*—and took a seat at the counter.

Introducing a restatement or explanation

Like a colon, a dash can be used to introduce an explanation or restatement in place of expressions such as *that is, in other words,* or *namely.* Begin the clause after the dash with a lowercase letter.

The reporter relentlessly pursued the woman—*he was determined to get her to make a statement.*

Although the colon and dash are frequently interchangeable in this function, the dash is less formal.

Dashes with commas

When you use dashes to set off interrupting elements in a sentence, omit commas.

She saw her sisters—*all five of them*—*standing* in front of the building.

NOT She saw her sisters—*all five of them*—, *standing* in front of the building.

Dashes with quotation marks

If a dash is not part of the quoted material, put it outside the quotation marks. Omit commas.

"He wants the money"—*I paused for effect*—"and he wants it now."

A dash can be used to indicate unfinished dialogue. Put the dash within the quotation marks and omit commas or periods.

"*Help! Help! I can't seem to*—" She fell to the ground, gasping for breath.

Problems with Dashes

If you like dashes, you may be tempted to use them too often. Dashes are more noticeable than commas. So remember a basic rule: Don't let a punctuation mark become a distraction.

When you type, don't confuse a dash with a hyphen. The hyphen is mainly used to break syllables of a word: *pre-existing*. A short dash (en dash –) is used with ranges (*April 1–5, pages 70–75*). A longer dash (em dash —) is typed as two hyphens with no space between them. Most word processing programs convert the two hyphens to a longer dash (see the following examples).

> Ms. Persinger--*the most important official in the city*--okayed the plan.
>
> OR Ms. Persinger—*the most important official in the city*—okayed the plan. (better)
>
> NOT Ms. Persinger-*the most important official in the city*-okayed the plan.

Uses of Parentheses

Parentheses are a pair of signs ( ) helpful in marking off text. You use parentheses in specific situations that can be covered by a few simple guidelines.

Setting off incidental information

Parentheses are used to enclose incidental or extra information, such as a passing comment, a minor example or addition, or a brief explanation. The writer may choose to put additional information within parentheses or to set off the text using dashes or commas. Again, overuse of parentheses or dashes can be distracting to readers.

> Some of the local store owners (*Mr. Kwan and Ms. Lawson, for example*) insisted that the street be widened.
>
> OR Some of the local store owners—*Mr. Kwan and Ms. Lawson, for example*—insisted that the street be widened.
>
> Roger Worthington (*a poorly drawn character in the novel*) reveals the secret in the last chapter.
>
> OR Roger Worthington, *a poorly drawn character in the novel,* reveals the secret in the last chapter.

Other punctuation marks with parentheses

Don't put any punctuation mark before parentheses, and put a comma after the closing parenthesis *only* if the sentence needs a comma anyway.

Use a pointed stick (*a pencil with the lead point broken off works well*) or a similar tool.

No comma appears before or after the parentheses. If you were to remove the parenthetical remark, the remaining sentence would not need a comma: *Use a pointed stick or a similar tool.*

Banging the wall and screaming (*unrestrained by his father, I might add*), Sam was acting like a brat.

In the preceding sentence, no comma appears before the parentheses. A comma follows the parentheses because if the parenthetical comment is removed, the rest of the sentence would require a comma: *Banging the wall and screaming, Sam was acting like a brat.*

Punctuation within parentheses

If your parentheses enclose a sentence-within-a-sentence, don't use a period within the parentheses. Do use a question mark or an exclamation mark if it is called for.

Mother love (*hers was fierce*) ruined the young boy's life.

They finally said (*why didn't they admit it earlier?*) that she had been there.

The wedding reception (*what a fiasco!*) ended abruptly.

If the parentheses enclose a complete sentence that can stand alone, place the period inside the closing parentheses.

(*Her father was the only one who didn't attend.*)

If the parentheses enclose a phrase that falls at the end of the sentence, place the closing punctuation outside the closing mark.

The only one who didn't attend was Mr. Jensen (*her father*).

Miscellaneous uses of parentheses

You should learn how to use parentheses in special situations. For example, use parentheses to enclose a date or a citation.

Sir William Walton (*1902–1983*) composed the oratorio *Belshazzar's Feast.*

According to the reports of her contemporaries, she was a mediocre critic and a worse artist (*Travis, 26–62*).

In scientific, business, or legal writing, parentheses are used to restate a number. However, in most writing, it is not justified, and it creates an overly official tone.

The bill is due and payable in *thirty* (*30*) days. (acceptable)

My grandfather knew my grandmother for *sixty* (*60*) years. (not appropriate)

When to use brackets

Brackets are a special case and are only used in specific situations. Use brackets to insert something into a sentence that is already enclosed in parentheses.

(Don't forget, however, that the joints will be filled with grout [*see page 46*].)

Also use brackets when you want to insert an explanatory word or note within a quotation.

"Bill and Melinda [*Griffin*] are two of my best customers," the street vendor bragged.

Problems with Parentheses

Like dashes, parentheses are punctuation marks with high visibility, so don't overuse them. If you find yourself putting too much information in parentheses, check the way you have organized your material. Generally, your writing should be straightforward, not filled with asides or passing comments.

Uses of Quotation Marks

Quotation marks are used to indicate the beginning and end of a quote. They tell the reader when you've used written material from other sources or direct speech.

Direct quotations

A direct quotation tells the reader when words are taken directly from another text or source.

Use quotation marks at the beginning and end of a direct quotation.

"*You are the last person on earth I'd ask,*" she told him.

When you are incorporating a short quotation into a paper or essay, use quotation marks and quote the wording exactly.

> As film critic Pauline Kael writes, "At his greatest, Jean Renoir expresses the beauty in our common humanity—the desires and hopes, the absurdities and follies, that we all, to one degree or another, share."

In a double-spaced paper, indent and single-space direct quotations that are longer than five typed lines. A long quotation should be preceded by a colon and does not need to be enclosed in quotation marks. See the example in the following section.

Quotations within quotations

Use single quotation marks within double ones to indicate a quotation within a quotation.

> "*My father began by saying, 'I refuse to listen to any excuses,*'" he told the psychiatrist.

If you are indenting and single spacing a long quotation, use the same punctuation marks that appear in the original passage. In this example, the writer is quoting a passage from the critic Martin Esslin, who in turn is quoting the playwright Ionesco.

> Martin Esslin describes Ionesco's attitude toward spontaneity in this passage:
>
> Ionesco regards spontaneity as an important creative element. "*I have no ideas before I write a play. I have them when I have written the play or while I am not writing at all. I believe that artistic creation is spontaneous. It certainly is so for me.*" But this does not mean that he considers his writing to be meaningless or without significance. On the contrary, the workings of the spontaneous imagination are a cognitive process, an exploration.

Miscellaneous uses of quotation marks

There are a few other situations that call for quotation marks.

To distance yourself from an offensive term or expression (quoting someone else).

> The disappointed body builder blamed the "*fat slobs*" who judged the contest.

To refer to a word as a word.

> She repeatedly used the term *"irregardless,"* not realizing that no such word exists.

To indicate a nickname written as part of a formal name.

> Ray *"Shorty"* Johannsen was the unanimous choice for committee chair.

To set off titles of poems, essays, and articles that are part of a longer work. (For this use, as for bibliographical and footnote information, check to see whether you are required to use a specific style guide for your writing.)

Problems with Quotation Marks

One of the biggest problems with quotation marks is knowing whether another type of punctuation, such as a period or comma, goes inside or outside the quotation marks. Here is a summary of rules that will help you avoid errors:

- Put **periods and commas** inside quotation marks, whether or not they are part of the quotation.

  > Her little sister said, "I want to go swimming."

  > "The pool opens tomorrow," he said.

- Put **question marks, exclamation marks, and dashes** inside quotation marks if they are part of the quotation.

  > His sister asked, "Is it hot enough to go swimming today?"

  > He screamed, "I don't want to go swimming!"

  > The last words we heard were, "I want to go—"

- Put question marks, exclamation marks, and dashes outside quotation marks if they are not part of the quotation.

- **Colons and semicolons** always go outside quotation marks.

  > On Monday the instructor said, "I'm grading your essays"; a week later, we still hadn't received our papers back.

  > The new tenant said, "I'll return the contract": a detailed rental agreement and explanation of the necessary damage deposit.

When using punctuation marks with quotation marks, remember to reserve quotation marks for direct quotations and for the other uses described in this chapter. Don't use quotation marks around the title of your paper. Don't use them to signal—and somehow justify—the use of clichés or slang expressions. Don't use them to indicate that you are being clever or funny. In fact, don't use them to call attention to your tone at all.

Uses of an Ellipsis

An **ellipsis** indicates that words have been omitted from a quotation. This mark consists of spaced periods.

A **three-dot ellipsis** indicates that you are omitting something from a sentence that continues after the ellipsis.

> He writes, "*The wise collector should probably just bite the bullet . . . and acquire both paintings.*"

The phrase "or mortgage the house" has been omitted from this quotation.

Use a **four-dot ellipsis** if you are omitting the last part of a quoted sentence that ends in a period, but the remaining words are still a complete thought. The first dot comes immediately after the sentence and functions as a period. The following three dots are spaced and indicate that material has been omitted. If the original sentence ended in a question mark or exclamation point, substitute that mark for the first dot.

> The author advises, "*In analyzing nonverbal signals, look at the total pattern of behavior rather than just one symbol. . . .*"

The phrase "before making a decision," which ended the sentence, has been omitted from this quotation.

You can also use the four-dot ellipsis whenever your quotation skips material and then goes on to a new sentence. But make sure that your four-dot ellipsis has an independent clause on each side of it.

> *The market researchers outlined several possible explanations for the drop in sales. . . . No matter how many ways they analyzed the data, the projections were negative.*

Chapter Check-Out

Questions

1. Choose the correct location for punctuation in the following sentences. If no punctuation is needed, write NP (No Punctuation) in the blank.

   a. Minh stated, "The results are in____"____
   b. The study revealed, "Wages are down . . .____"____
   c. He cried, "Hold the door____"____
   d. Bridget asked, "When will we stop____"____
   e. "Now is the time____"____we must act today____

2. Note which sentences are correct as is and which sentences could be corrected by the addition of a dash or parentheses.

   a. Lost in the museum the second one we visited Mark never panicked.
   b. Even though Carlton was well qualified, he lost the election.
   c. My cousin Sara is a dancer a ballet dancer.
   d. Mrs. Millick was rude and not for the first time to my wife.

3. Note which sentences show correct or incorrect use of quotation marks.

   a. The term "generation Y" was coined recently.
   b. As the movie ended, he whispered, "Let's go."
   c. Dr. Schwartz cited a study that claimed "Life exists on Mars."
   d. Claire read aloud to the girls' team, "When playing basketball, the key is individual endurance. . . . "

Answers

1. **a.** Minh stated, "The results are in."NP

   b. The study revealed, "Wages are down. . .."NP

   c. He cried, "Hold the door!" NP

   d. Bridget asked, "When will we stop?" NP

   e. "Now is the time NP"; we must act today

2. **a.** Lost in the museum—the second one we visited—Mark never panicked.

   b. correct as is

   c. My cousin Sara is a dancer—a ballet dancer.

   d. Mrs. Millick was rude (and not for the first time) to my wife.

3. **a.** correct

   b. correct

   c. incorrect (Dr. Schwartz cited a study that claimed life exists on Mars.)

   d. correct

Chapter 11

IDIOMS, CLICHÉS, JARGON, SLANG, EUPHEMISMS, AND WORDINESS

Chapter Check-In

❑ Recognize idioms and clichés

❑ Avoid jargon, slang, and buzzwords

❑ Identify euphemisms and doublespeak

❑ Learn to detect wordy and redundant language

As a writer, you must choose each word carefully. Unclear or careless language affects your ability to communicate. It is important for you to recognize words or expressions that weaken your message in order to avoid them in your writing.

Idioms are expressions that do not have a literal meaning; rather, they establish their connotation by how they are used in speech. **Clichés** are expressions that are so common and overused that they fail to impart any real impact on your sentence. **Jargon** is the specialized, often technical, language that is used by people in a particular field, profession, or social group. **Slang** is the informal language of conversation, text messages, and other casual social communication among friends. **Euphemisms** are milder words or phrases used to blunt the effect of more direct or unpleasant words or phrases. If you know when to use or avoid these expressions, your writing will be more effective. (See the Appendix: Frequently Confused Words.)

Idioms

An **idiom** is a commonly used phrase or expression that doesn't follow the usual language patterns or that has a meaning other than the literal.

Phrases that, when dissected, don't seem to make much sense, are often idiomatic. For example, when you read "They can't *come up with* the answer," or "The director *stood up for* herself," or "The play ended *with a bang,*" you probably know what the writer means. But if you look up the definition of each word in these phrases, the meaning of the expression as a whole does not make sense.

Idioms aren't something you memorize. If English is your native language, you already know thousands of idioms, so you don't question what they mean. But if you try to learn the idioms of another language, or if you are trying to learn English, you'll find that idioms can be a real challenge.

Figurative idioms

Figurative idioms are expressions so common you don't question their source: *let the cat out of the bag, he has a monkey on his back, it's the straw that broke the camel's back, you're splitting hairs, the ball's in your court,* and so on. Many figurative idioms have become clichés and empty of true meaning. You can use them occasionally—but don't overuse them.

Prepositional idioms

The most common idiom is an expression that depends on the choice of a particular preposition. The choice may seem arbitrary. For example, why do we say "She *put up with* him" rather than "She *put on* with him"? *"At home"* rather than *"in home"*? Why is it *"sick of* him*"* rather than "sick *from* him"? Why do we get *in* a car but *on* a boat? There is no logical reason; the expressions are idiomatic. Notice in addition that many words take different prepositions to form different idioms. For example, to *wait on someone* is different from *to wait for someone.*

Prepositional idioms don't follow rules you can memorize. Fortunately, you can usually rely on your ear and your experience. When you're in doubt about the right preposition for an expression, check a dictionary. The entry for a word sometimes gives you a phrase showing which preposition to use. When the word is associated with several idioms, they are often listed at the end of the entry.

Examples of prepositional idioms

Although far from complete, this list illustrates the importance of prepositions in forming idioms.

accountable for (responsible for)—I am *accountable for* the errors in the book.

accountable to (answerable to someone)—I am *accountable to* the board of directors.

adapt from (a model)—He *adapted* the design *from* one he had seen in Europe.

adapt to (a situation, an environment)—The children soon *adapted to* the new school.

agree on or upon (something)—We *agreed on* a date for the meeting.

agree to (do something)—We *agree to* pay the damages.

agree with (people, opinions)—The women who were polled *agreed with* the judge.

annoyed at or with (a person)—The physician was *annoyed at* her for the interruption.

annoyed by (something)—The physician was *annoyed by* the constant interruptions.

assist at (an event)—He *assisted at* the service.

assist with (someone or something)—Mr. Nguyen *assisted with* the refreshments and the flowers.

contend for (a position, a prize)—The candidates have *contended for* the office twice.

contend with (an obstacle)—The candidate has to *contend with* his lack of personal charm.

depart for (*not* to, a destination)—They *depart for* Canada tomorrow.

depart from (a destination, a tradition)—They *departed from* their routine today.

grateful for (a benefit)—I am *grateful for* my musical talent.

grateful to (a person)—I am *grateful to* you for the help.

impatient at (a delay)—They were *impatient at* having to wait so long.

impatient for (a result)—We are *impatient for* an answer from the administration.

impatient with (a person)—He was *impatient with* the clerk.

part from (leave)—I *parted from* the group early this year.

part with (a possession)—I *parted with* the Volvo reluctantly.

Clichés

Clichés are trite, overused expressions, many of which rely on figurative language. In the beginning, an expression is a fresh way of saying something. Although it's hard to believe, *pretty as a picture, old as the hills, sharp as a tack,* and *smart as a whip* were once new and exciting comparisons. But through overuse, they've become tiresome, and most writers avoid them. Other examples turn up everywhere from online chat and social networks to newspapers, magazines, and television. For example, someone may be *following his dream,* while someone else may be trying to *burst his bubble.* Sometimes *what you see is what you get,* but other times you meet people who have *a hidden agenda.* Watch out for *real-life superheroes, unsung heroes, human dynamos, living legends,* people who *push the panic button,* people who *live in glass houses,* and even *the man on the street.*

Along with stale figures of speech are phrases that have been used so often they are clichés: *all bent out of shape, axe to grind, contributing factor, first and foremost, grave danger, go belly up, get an earful, grieving widow, grisly murder, in the final analysis, integral part, once and for all, one step closer, read between the lines, raw deal, the be-all and end-all, tried and true, vital role, unforeseen obstacles,* and so on. These trendy phrases appear and spread quickly, then become overused just as quickly; so avoid them in your writing.

Mixing clichés

A television reporter described a man as *having signed his own death knell.* Her error illustrates a mix of clichés. The reporter no doubt meant *signed his own death warrant,* an overused expression that means *to cause one's own destruction through a particular act.* But she confused that expression with another, *sounding the death knell,* which means *to announce the end of something,* or, *to cause the end of something,* as in "Cutting off the funds *sounded the death knell* for the struggling program." Literally, a knell is the sound of a bell tolling, as at a funeral. Obviously, it's not possible to sign a knell.

Avoiding clichés

Before you use any expression or description that sounds familiar, think about it carefully. Is there a better, more descriptive or precise way to say what you want to say? For example, it is stronger to say that he was *enraged,* rather than he was *hopping mad* or *mad as a wet hen.* Whatever you do, don't use a cliché and then apologize for it: *Pardon my use of the cliché, but it's true that all that glitters is not gold.* The apology does nothing but draw attention to the tired, overused expression.

Using clichés in new ways

On rare occasions, clichés get new life with a witty turn or a surprising application. For example, baseball legend Yogi Berra twisted a standard expression when he said, "When you come to a fork in the road, take it"; and civil rights activist H. Rap Brown did it with his line "Violence is as American as cherry pie." If you can use a trite expression or cliché in a new, surprising way, you are overcoming the expression's predictability. As with all attempts at cleverness, be sure that you're achieving the desired effect and not just making a bad joke.

Jargon and Buzzwords

Jargon is the specialized language of a particular field, trade, social or cultural group, occupation, or profession—information technology, the military, government, psychology, economics, mathematics, biology, medicine, and so on. When you are writing a paper in a particular field, you can use these specialized terms that are accepted and understood in that field. **Buzzwords** are terms that have spread beyond their original field, and people outside the occupation often use the words imprecisely or pretentiously, for example: *downsize, cutting edge, holistic, benchmarking, paradigm, synergy, tipping point, off-shoring, next generation.*

Negative connotations of jargon

The term *jargon* has other negative connotations. Jargon can seem like gibberish to most people. When a special term arises because it describes or categorizes something in a helpful way, it is acceptable. But when jargon becomes a way of making something sound more scientific, technical, or complex than it really is, it should be avoided. Jargon is sometimes merely doublespeak, and it is also often responsible for wordy, heavy-handed sentences.

Avoiding jargon and buzzwords

In your writing, avoid using specialized terms from a particular field unless you are writing in or about that field. For example, you can talk about *computers interfacing* more appropriately than about *people interfacing. Risk-averse investments* is a tolerable phrase; *risk-averse children* should be changed to *children who are afraid to take risks.* Specialized terms can have distinct meanings within a field; if you borrow them to describe other phenomena, you may be making a mistake. At the very least, you may confuse the reader.

Slang Expressions

Electronic communication helps to spread slang, jargon, and buzzwords around the world. Popular words and expressions appear and disappear quickly. Advertisers, politicians, commentators, bloggers, business people, and educators can start and spread trendy, slang expressions, for example: *dysfunctional, parenting, syndrome, ethnicity, viable, entrepreneurial, crunch time, proactive, tipping point, walk the walk,* and *cutting edge,* in addition to nouns used as verbs, such as *dialogue, leverage, author, impact,* and *Google.*

Most people who write formal reports, research papers, academic assignments, and essays avoid slang and buzzwords. For example, in an analysis of the political, military, and economic conflicts in the Middle East, it would be inappropriate to talk about *heavy-duty* problems or describe the situation as *the pits.* Writing about the injuries of accident victims, you wouldn't say *they grossed me out* or that the paramedics' response was *totally awesome.* You wouldn't describe the president of Argentina as *hot, cool,* or *adorable.* Although you might use these expressions when talking to a friend, in your formal writing, you must use words that are appropriate to the purpose, audience, and tone of your written piece. (See Chapter 12, "How to Begin a Writing Assignment," for information about evaluating the purpose, audience, and tone of your writing.)

Sometimes slang or jargon can be used appropriately in writing. In dialogue, for instance, it can characterize a speaker. In a humorous piece, a slang word like *freak* (as in *neat freak*) might work. Remember that slang words can quickly become outdated—the *cat's pajamas, keen, swell, hip, groovy,* and so on.

Euphemisms

A **euphemism** is a mild or roundabout word or phrase used in place of one considered painful or offensive—for example, *golden years* for *old age* or *economically disadvantaged* for *poor.* Other kinds of euphemisms, rather than covering up, inflate or magnify, making something sound more important or grander than it is: *technical representative* for *salesperson,* for example, or *handcrafted* for *handmade.*

People use euphemisms to protect themselves and others from the harsh realities of life—*senior citizen* for *old person, discomfort* for *pain, pass away* for *die.* People also use euphemisms like *sleeping together, having a relationship,* or *going to the bathroom* to be polite. Terms such as *idiot, imbecile, moron,* and *crippled* were once neutral, but now these words are regarded as offensive and insensitive. Euphemisms often deal with profanity, body parts, bodily functions, sex, death, murder, societal taboos, superstitions, or other issues that may not be considered fit for polite conversation or writing. In social settings, euphemisms can be justified as preserving propriety.

People also use euphemisms to cover up or disguise motives and events. For example, the phrase *a strategic movement to the rear* sounds less humiliating than *retreat*. A *preemptive strike* is much more acceptable than a *sneak attack*.

Euphemisms and **doublespeak** are closely related. A phrase in doublespeak, like a euphemism, is a roundabout way of saying something. It can be hard to figure out what a statement in doublespeak means, which is what its originators had in mind. Doublespeak is almost always intended to confuse or deceive.

Avoiding euphemisms

Socially, you may need to use some euphemisms if you don't want to offend someone or be thought of as insensitive. In your writing, however, strive to be direct. Resist the temptation to be overly polite, to cover up hard facts, or to inflate something by using a euphemistic term.

Examples of euphemisms

Euphemisms are everywhere, and more are born every day. This brief list should make you think about the various reasons they exist.

au naturel, in the buff: naked

categorical inaccuracy: lie

collateral damage: in a bombing, civilian casualties and destruction of civilian buildings

comfort station: public toilet

(the) departed: the dead person; died

disincentive: penalty; reprisal

disinformation: lie

enhanced interrogation techniques: torture

ethnic cleansing: eliminating people from racial or national backgrounds different from your own; *eliminating* is itself a euphemism for deporting, or killing

fabricate: make up

freedom fighters: rebels fighting a government seen as hostile to one's own interests

friendly fire: artillery fire from one's own forces that accidentally or mistakenly wounds or kills someone on one's own side

furlough (employees): lay off

gaming: gambling

gentlemen's club: strip club

imbibe, feeling no pain (and many others): drink, getting drunk

inventory leakage: theft

job action: a strike or work slowdown

neutralize: to take out of action, to kill

out-source: for cost-saving purposes, to send work to workers outside of the organization (sometimes far away) to whom no benefits need be paid rather than hire full-time workers with benefits

pacify: to repress or destroy an enemy

personal flotation device: life preserver on an airplane or boat

preowned: used, for example, used car

relocation center: an American-style prison camp used to hold Japanese-Americans during World War II

revenue enhancements: taxes

reverse engineering: taking something apart to see how it works and then copying it

stress-producing stimulus: electric shock

surreptitious entry: break-in

visually challenged: blind; *challenged* has become part of a host of euphemisms both serious and humorous (for example, *vertically challenged* for *short*)

Wordiness

A **redundant expression** says the same thing twice, and **doublespeak** avoids getting directly to the point. Both are examples of wordy expressions. Other such expressions use more than one word when one word is simpler and more direct—for example, using the phrase *in the vicinity of* instead of *near*.

Redundant expressions

In writing, **redundancy** means conveying the same meaning twice. Like other kinds of wordiness, redundancy makes writing seem cluttered. Sometimes people use redundant expressions because they don't know the precise definition of a word. For example, *close proximity* is redundant because *proximity* by itself means *nearness*. Ask yourself: Is there any other kind of nearness than close nearness? Other times people use redundant expressions because they don't pay attention to what they are writing: *small in size, few in number, or red in color.*

Examples of redundant expressions

Look for redundant expressions, and you'll find them everywhere. Tables 11-1 and 11-2 present short lists. When you write, check your drafts to make sure you are getting the full value of the words you choose and not adding unnecessary ones.

Table 11-1   Redundant Adjectives, Adverbs, and Nouns

advance planning	free gift	sad lament
brief summary	fundamental basis	safe haven
close intimates	future ahead	same identical
close scrutiny	human artifact	sudden impulse
completely unanimous	Jewish rabbi	true fact
consensus of opinion	more better	two opposites
currently at this time	new innovation	unexpected surprise
empty void	now pending	unimportant triviality
end result	past history	wealthy millionaire
exact same	present incumbent	yearly annual
famous celebrity	rejected outcast	vast majority

Table 11-2   Redundant Verbs

advance forward	leave from	retreat back
continue on	lower down	return back
cooperate together	overexaggerate	revert back
enter into (buildings)	proceed forward	share in common
join together	raise up	share together

There is, there are, it is expressions

Many wordy expressions occur in sentences starting with *there is, there are,* or *it is* constructions. Writing that uses a clear subject and action verbs is less redundant, clearer, and more direct.

> *There is* a famous author who lives on my block.
> BETTER A famous author lives on my block.

> *There are* many people who play Scrabble online.
> BETTER Many people play Scrabble online.

> *There are* some animals that thrive in arctic temperatures.
> BETTER Some animals thrive in arctic temperatures.

> *It is* rarely *the case that* people refuse to help.
> BETTER People rarely refuse to help.

> *It is a fact that* most of us like to be praised.
> BETTER Most of us like to be praised.

Overused intensifiers

Intensifiers are words intended to add force to what you say: *very, absolutely, positively, really, quite,* and so on. Sometimes you need them, but more often these are empty words that add nothing. You can prune them without affecting your tone or meaning. Here are some examples.

> Roosevelt, *certainly a quite active president,* refused to give in to his handicap.
> BETTER Roosevelt, *an active president,* refused to give in to his handicap.

She *positively expects* to win this election.
BETTER She *expects* to win this election.

The results were *very surprising*.
BETTER The results were surprising.

Examples of wordy expressions

New wordy expressions are created every day. Check your writing for similar roundabout ways of saying what you mean.

after the conclusion of = **after:** *After* the concert we left NOT *After the conclusion of* the concert we left.

all of = **all:** *All* the boys came NOT *All of* the boys came.

any and all = **any** or **all:** We appreciate *any* suggestions NOT We appreciate *any and all* suggestions.

at the present moment, at this point in time = **now:** We are looking for a solution *now* NOT We are looking for a solution *at the present moment.*

by means of = **by:** He came *by* car NOT He came *by means* of a car.

due to the fact that = **because:** *Because* he called, we waited NOT *Due to the fact that* he called, we waited.

for the purpose of (+ gerund) = **to:** The meeting is *to* discuss plans NOT The meeting is *for the purpose of* discussing plans.

he is a man who is = **he is:** *He is* admired NOT *He is a man who is* admired.

In a place where = **where:** They lived *where* no trees grew NOT They lived *in a place where* no trees grew.

in connection with = **about:** He telephoned *about* the rally NOT He telephoned *in connection with* the rally.

in order to = **to:** He said this *to* help you NOT He said this *in order to* help you.

in spite of the fact that = **although** or **though:** *Although* she agreed, she was sad NOT *In spite of the fact that* she agreed, she was sad.

in the near future = **soon:** We'll see you *soon* NOT We'll see you *in the near future.*

in view of the fact that = **because:** *Because* she helped us, we won NOT *In view of the fact that* she helped us, we won.

is located in = is in: Ventura County *is in* California NOT Ventura County *is located in* California.

on the part of = by: A suggestion *by* the consultant helped NOT A suggestion *on the part of* the consultant helped.

owing to the fact that = because: *Because* he was here, we stayed NOT *Owing to the fact that* he was here, we stayed.

rarely ever = rarely: She *rarely* speaks to a large group NOT She *rarely ever* speaks to a large group.

the fact is that, the truth is that = often omit altogether: You are the right candidate NOT *The fact is that* you are the right candidate.

which was when = when: I spoke with him yesterday *when* he called NOT I spoke with him yesterday, *which was when* he called.

with the exception of = except: I like all sports *except* boxing NOT I like all sports *with the exception of* boxing.

Chapter Check-Out

Questions

1. Choose the correct idiom to complete the following sentences.

    a. Carlos was reconciled *to/with* the biologist, who was his mentor.

    b. Ryan agreed *on/to/with* sharing the cost of the vacation.

    c. Clearly frustrated, the diver was annoyed *at/by* the low scores from the two judges.

2. Yes or no: Do the following sentences contain an example of either jargon or slang?

    a. It's so awesome to wear those colors this year.

    b. My hard drive crashed last night because the graphics card was overloaded.

    c. The results of her findings will have long-lasting repercussions throughout the psychiatric community.

3. Underline the cliché in the following sentences.

    a. The Olympic weight lifter was as strong as an ox.

    b. Sharp as a tack, Rosita never lost a chess match.

    c. After the initial questions, the inquest was smooth sailing for him.

4. Note which of the following statements are wordy and which are direct.

    a. Jess Luna is the man who ran for president.

    b.   There are several good reasons why you should visit Prague.

    c.   We stayed home because of the fact that Theresa was ill.

    d.   There are several close friends arriving late.

5. Match the wordy expression to its simpler synonym. You may use one complement more than once.

a.	By means of	because
b.	In the very near future	except
c.	Due to the fact that	now
d.	As a result of	by
e.	At the current time	soon
f.	With the lone exception of	

Answers

1. a. with; **b.** to; **c.** by

2. a. yes; **b.** yes; **c.** no

3. a. strong as an ox; **b.** sharp as a tack; **c.** smooth sailing

4. a. wordy: Jess Luna ran for president.
    b. direct
    c. wordy: We stayed home because Theresa was ill.
    d. wordy: Several close friends are arriving late.

5. a. by; **b.** soon; **c.** because; **d.** because; **e.** now; **f.** except

Chapter 12

HOW TO BEGIN A WRITING ASSIGNMENT

Chapter Check-In

❏ Define the writing process

❏ Determine your audience

❏ Select a topic

❏ Create a thesis

❏ Avoid fallacies in logic

Writing is a process. Good writers follow a formula that consists of prewriting, writing, revising, editing, and proofreading. This process allows their work to emerge in a series of small, manageable steps.

The first step is to define the purpose of your writing. Select a topic that is narrow enough to be explained within your page limitations. A thesis, unlike a topic, is a single statement that makes an assertion about a topic. It is usually placed in the introduction of an essay. Often, a thesis sentence gives the reader a clear overview of the essay content by stating the main ideas.

Steps in Writing

Although it is a process, writing doesn't progress as neatly from one step to the next as does, for example, baking cookies or changing a tire. Roughly speaking, when you write, you do the following:

1. Decide on a topic (or have a topic assigned to you).
2. Explore ideas about the topic through thinking, reading, listening, and so on.

3. Formulate a thesis or main idea, and decide what points you want to make to support it.

4. Select details and examples from reading, research, and personal experience.

5. Decide on the order in which you'll present your ideas and examples.

6. Write a first draft.

7. Edit and revise the first draft for content, style, and writing mechanics.

8. Write a final draft.

At any time during this process, you may need to stop and go back several steps. For example, when you're selecting details and examples, you may realize your topic is too broad or your thesis statement is weak. Or when organizing main points, you may see that the thesis you *thought* you were developing isn't the one that you *are* developing. Often the act of writing itself generates new ideas you may want to pursue. Even as late as your final draft, you may decide that the organization isn't working, or you may spot a flaw in your argument that causes you to throw out much of what you've written and rework the rest.

Writing is not a straight-line task; it's more of a back-and-forward activity. Take that into account when deciding how long you'll need to finish a writing assignment. Allow plenty of time for each step in the process.

Types of Writing

The writing you're required to do in your lifetime varies—for example, timed writings and essay questions on exams; autobiographical essays for college applications; high-school and college papers on a variety of subjects; and business letters, proposals, memos, and reports related to your work. In most of your writing you'll do one of the following:

■ Describe a person, place, or thing

■ Tell a story or recount an incident or event

■ Report information

■ Provide instructions or explain a process

■ Argue a position, prove a point, or persuade

■ Analyze or critique something—a text, theory, situation, or event

The techniques you use will overlap. For example, if you're writing a descriptive essay about your Aunt Stephanie, you might narrate an incident that reveals her personality.

Many college writing assignments focus on argument and analysis. But within an essay arguing a position, you might use descriptive and narrative techniques. In a paper arguing for or against capital punishment, for example, you might recount the steps of an execution, or narrate an incident of lethal injection. In choosing your approach to any writing task, you must clearly understand and be guided by the purpose of your writing.

Understanding Your Assignment

If you're given a writing assignment, fulfilling it is your main purpose. If you don't understand the assignment, talk to your instructor. If you're asked to write a paper analyzing how an author's techniques contribute to his theme, and if you describe the theme thoroughly but don't discuss the techniques, then you've failed to fulfill the assignment. Or if in a psychology class you're asked to compare and contrast two theories about selective amnesia, and you write five pages on one of the theories and only half a page on the other, you probably haven't done what is required.

In many ways, writing on the job is similar to writing for a class assignment. For example, if you need to write a testing protocol for a new product, you should include such elements as a detailed description of the testing samples and the control group, the conditions of testing, materials and equipment, all the steps of the tests, relevant formulas and equations, and the methods to be used in evaluating results. If after the testing your manager asks for a summary of the results, you should provide it as clearly, honestly, and succinctly as you can. You may need to include a brief explanation of the tests, but you don't want to overdo the details. Whether you're writing in school or at work, make sure you understand your task, and then focus on achieving your purpose.

Understanding Your Audience

Before you begin, think about your **audience.** For whom are you writing? A reader is on the receiving end of your writing, and you should keep that reader in mind.

Student writers sometimes think that their audience is an instructor who will be impressed by big words and long sentences. But most teachers know good, clear writing when they see it. And they can easily distinguish between solid content and inflated trivia. If you have little to say but dress it up in overblown prose with perfect punctuation, you won't fare as well as someone who has something substantive to say and says it clearly, even with a few mechanical errors.

The purpose of your writing and the audience for whom you're writing are closely related. If you're writing a letter to a snowboarding magazine praising a new board, you'll use different language and tone than you would in a college research paper about the European Union's gradual move toward a single currency. Though both audiences will be interested in what you write and want to understand it, they'll expect and respond to different styles.

Think carefully about your audience before you begin. Here are some questions to consider:

- **Are you writing for people in a particular field, such as psychology, literature, engineering, or genetics?** Can you assume the reader has knowledge of the terminology and concepts you'll use, or do you need to define them in the paper? Will you need to provide extensive background information on the subject, or will a summary be enough?

- **What expectations does your audience have?** An audience of marine biologists will have different expectations from an article on marine biology than will a general audience, for example.

- **Are you writing for someone who insists on certain writing practices or who has pet peeves?** One instructor may require a five-paragraph essay; another may forbid the use of intentional sentence fragments. Be aware of requirements or restrictions related to grammar, punctuation, and usage.

- **What is the reading level of your audience?** Instructions and explanations written for sixth-graders shouldn't include college-level vocabulary, for example.

- **Are you writing for an audience that is likely to agree or disagree with your point of view?** Consider this question if you're writing an argumentative or persuasive piece. It can make a difference in the language you select, the amount of proof you offer, and the tone you use. For example, an editorial for a small-town paper on the importance of family values is less likely to encounter resistance from readers than an editorial on legalizing drugs.

Guidelines for Choosing a Topic

Often you're assigned a topic to write about or asked to choose among several topics. When you can choose your own topic, keep the following points in mind:

■ **Choose a topic that's appropriate to the length of your paper.** Students often pick topics that are too broad to be adequately covered. Narrow topics lead to close observation, while broad topics lead to overgeneralization. If you're writing a five-page paper, don't write on the history of women's rights; instead, write about one incident in the history of women's rights. Even a personal or descriptive essay will be better if you choose a narrow topic—your childhood in a small town, for example, rather than your childhood, or your uncle's barn rather than the Midwest.

■ **Avoid a topic that will tempt you to summarize rather than to discuss or analyze.** Don't choose *the plot of Macbeth* but *how the final scene of Macbeth illustrates the play's theme.* The second topic is narrower and less likely to lead to summary. When considering a topic, ask yourself if it can lead to a reasonable thesis.

■ **Choose a topic that interests you.** If you don't care about limiting cigarette advertising, don't select it as a topic for a persuasive essay. You'll have more to say, and you'll write better, on something you care about. Generally, if you choose a topic that is interesting to you, then your reader will find it interesting too.

■ **If your assignment requires research, choose a topic on which you can find material.** Even when you aren't writing a research paper, make sure you select a subject that you can develop with sufficient details.

■ **After you've picked a topic, don't be afraid to change it if it isn't working out.** Instructors would rather you write a good essay than that you grind out pages on something that was a poor choice.

Topic vs. thesis

Don't confuse a topic with a main idea or thesis. The topic provides the subject; the thesis makes an assertion about that subject. Here are a few examples of topics that might be assigned to a college student:

1. Compare and contrast X's poem "To a Wolf" with Y's poem "The Happy Meercat." Consider both theme and technique.

2. Discuss the following statement: "No matter how much we may deplore human rights violations in China, the United States should not impose sanctions on the Chinese government." Do you agree or disagree? Support your opinion.

3. Analyze Shakespeare's use of clothing imagery in King Lear.

4. Describe an incident in your life that caused you to change an opinion or attitude.

5. "The Civil War had much more to do with economics than with morality." Do you agree or disagree with this statement? Support your opinion.

Topics 2 and 5 ask the writer to argue a position. A sentence expressing that position is a **thesis** statement. A thesis statement for the second topic might be: *Imposing sanctions on China would be a mistake because it would hurt the American economy, because sanctions are notoriously unsuccessful as a way to force change, and because the United States should not interfere in the internal policies of other countries.*

While the other topics don't ask the writer to take a position, the writer should still formulate a thesis. A thesis statement for the first bullet might be: *Although both poet X and poet Y show appreciation for their subjects, poet X's "To a Wolf" symbolizes the separation between humans and other animals, while poet Y's "The Happy Meercat" symbolizes the connection between all living things.* With this thesis statement, the writer makes a point about the topic and sets up a direction for developing the content of the essay.

Writing a thesis statement

When you write a paper that will, for example, analyze a literary work, compare theories, identify causes or effects, or argue a position, you should be able to write a thesis statement. You can refine and improve it as you go along, but try to begin with a one-sentence statement. A thesis statement can help you steer a straight course and avoid digression.

Don't be satisfied with weak generalities that fail to zero in on your main point. The following are examples of pseudo-thesis statements:

- Poets X and Y make important points about animals in their poems "To a Wolf" and "The Happy Meercat."

- People hold different opinions as to whether it is wise to impose sanctions on China because of their human rights violations.

- Shakespeare uses quite a bit of clothing imagery in *King Lear*.

None of these statements provides a clear direction for an essay because the assertions they make are too vague. A better thesis statement for the third example might be: *Clothing images in King Lear reflect the development of Lear from a man blinded by appearances to a man able to face the naked truth.* Remember that creating a thesis statement is important to the way you approach your topic and will help you direct your thinking and writing.

Avoiding Fallacies

As you write, be careful to avoid logic fallacies and ideological reasoning that would undermine the focus of your topic. **Logic fallacies** are errors in reasoning or connecting ideas. As a writer, you should avoid these logical errors in your own writing, and watch for them in the opinions and arguments of others—especially when you are doing research. Common fallacies include:

- **Ad hominem:** Also known as name-calling, this fallacy is a direct or indirect attack on a person.

  Bob can't be right because he is an idiot.

- **Bandwagon/celebrity appeal:** This fallacy implies that the reader should agree with a premise because a majority or a well-known person agrees with the premise.

  Everyone recognizes this bill will help our children.

- **Either/or reasoning:** This fallacy assumes that there can be only one cause or one solution in an issue.

  The only way to keep our children safe is to ban video games.

- **Slippery slope:** This fallacy assumes that because one minor fact is true, then a larger premise must be too, without any further proof.

  Congressman Smith voted against tax increases last week; therefore, Congressman Smith will always be against tax increases.

- **Ad populum:** This fallacy bases its argument on emotional appeals rather than facts from reliable sources.

  All true Americans want to ban this book.

- **Circular reasoning:** This fallacy presents a restatement of the problem itself as a cause of the problem.

  There are not enough parking spaces because there are too many cars.

Ideological reasoning is the use of cultural, religious, or moral values and beliefs to prove a position. While there is nothing wrong with making personal judgments, you should be aware that your audience might not share your ideological views. To reach the greatest number of readers, avoid making ideological reasons the foundation of your arguments.

Identifying the Main Idea

Narratives and personal essays require a central idea to help focus and direct your writing. For example, consider this topic: *Describe an incident in your life that caused you to change an opinion or attitude.* Before you begin writing, create a sentence that will both identify the incident and describe the change it caused. Here are some examples of main-idea statements.

- The divorce of my parents when I was seven changed my view that adults were infallible and always in control of their own lives.

- When I was eight, my cat became ill and died. I began to mistrust doctors' reassurances—a mistrust that has remained with me ever since.

- Changing high schools when I was fifteen made me realize for the first time that the fear of an experience is often worse than the reality.

Chapter Check-Out
Questions

1. Identify the problems with the following thesis statements.
   a. World religions are remarkably similar.
   b. Gun control is the only way to stop violence in schools.
   c. All parents who home-school their children agree that television has destroyed the cohesion of the American family.
   d. Brad should not be president of the Garden Club because he is a jerk.
   e. Rock music is bad because it is against my religion.

2. Identify the following as a topic or a thesis.
   a. Medieval harp music performed in Italy
   b. HIV-AIDS research on patients who were diagnosed before 1985
   c. Using smokeless tobacco should be banned in public places.
   d. HIV-AIDS funding is insufficient to meet the needs of researchers.

3. Identify whether the following statements about writing are true or false.
   a. Writing is a process.
   b. All writing is done for one purpose.
   c. Writers should analyze their audience before they begin writing.
   d. Research paper topics should be chosen based upon what will impress an instructor.
   e. A thesis is a topic spelled out in a complete sentence.
   f. A thesis statement should avoid fallacies in logic.

Answers

1. a. Unless you are writing a book, this topic is much too broad.

   b. This is a fallacy because it assumes that there is only one solution.

   c. This is a fallacy because it is based on an emotional appeal rather than facts.

   d. This is a fallacy because it is name-calling.

   e. This is a fallacy because it argues solely from an ideological position that not all readers may share.

2. a. topic; b. topic; c. thesis; d. thesis

3. a. true; b. false; c. true; d. false; e. false; f. true

Chapter 13

HOW TO RESEARCH AND ORGANIZE YOUR WRITING

Chapter Check-In

❑ Research a topic effectively

❑ Organize ideas to support a thesis

❑ Plan the essay

Once you have narrowed your topic and established a working thesis, you can start researching your essay. Begin by writing what you know about the topic before you go to the library or search the Internet. Generally, the source of information that is assumed to be common knowledge does not have to be cited as a source. However, you must cite the source of all quotations and ideas that come from another writer. While paraphrasing is a valuable way to summarize long passages or ideas from other writers, you must still cite the original source of your information.

Write an outline to help focus and develop the main ideas which support or explain your thesis. You can organize your ideas in a variety of spatial or chronological ways. Although a detailed written outline may seem like extra work, it is an essential tool for writing a good first draft. Starting with an outline will help you stay focused, which saves time later. (See Chapter 14, "Writing: From Introduction to Conclusion," for more details about how to outline.)

Finding Examples and Evidence

Once you have a topic, begin thinking of what you'll say. Write a thesis statement that clearly states your main idea. A thesis statement will help organize your thinking and direct your research.

Before you start writing, take notes on the topic. For personal essays, write down your thoughts, observations, memories, and experiences. When analyzing a text, take notes or underline significant sections. For most other essays, read materials to find details, examples, and illustrations to support your main idea. If you want to use quotations, write them down accurately. Remember that you'll need to cite the source of facts, ideas, or quotations, so be sure to write down bibliographical information in your notes.

Some of the information you write down will probably never appear in your essay. Your notes might include questions that occur to you as you read, related areas to explore, or reminders to check further on certain points. This preparation stage will not only help ensure that you have examples and evidence, but it will also help you think in more detail about your topic and thesis.

Brainstorming, taking notes, and outlining

Begin the process by free writing on the computer. Think about your topic, and for about 10 minutes, write down whatever comes to mind. Later, you can import parts of this file into your first draft. Take notes on the computer, too, being sure to include the information you'll need to cite references. The writer is responsible for accurately noting information sources—whether using parenthetical documentation (citations within the text of the paper), footnotes or endnotes, a references page, or a bibliography. There are many styles of documentation, but you'll save time if you start a list of sources early in the writing process. You can add to and rearrange the list later.

Consider creating a formal outline on the computer, using Roman numerals for headings, alpha characters for first-level subheadings, and so on. If you go back into your outline to add a heading or subheading, the program will automatically update your outline designations. Outlining on the computer will let you experiment with different organizational plans.

Using the Internet for research

With a computer, you can access thousands of documents and databases. You can call up current and historical newspaper articles and photos, interviews and blogs, journal articles and abstracts, encyclopedias and dictionaries, and much more. Through the Internet, you can view library archival materials and instantly call up information posted by educational institutions, businesses, professional organizations, civic and religious groups, museums, media outlets, government agencies, international organizations, and individuals from around the world. In fact, so much information is available online that you may feel overwhelmed.

Before you use the Internet to do serious research, it's a good idea to get some training. Librarians can guide you to reliable, credible sources of information on your topic. How-to books and classes can also steer you in the right direction. Search engines and Internet directories can help you navigate, but you must critically evaluate the validity of each source. Just because a person or group publishes information on a Web site doesn't mean the information is accurate, truthful, or current.

When you use information from electronic sources in a paper, consult a current style guide (such as the *MLA Handbook for Writers of Research Papers*) for the correct way to cite it in parenthetical documentation, footnotes, a references page, or a bibliography.

The Importance of Specific Details

A frequent mistake in writing is failing to provide specific examples, evidence, or details to support an idea or thesis. In an essay about a poem, for example, it isn't enough to say that the author's language creates a dark, gloomy atmosphere. You should identify particular words and images that demonstrate this effect. In an essay arguing that magnet schools in cities improve education for minority students, you must provide evidence—statistics, anecdotes, and so on. If your assignment is to write an essay on the statement, *We learn more from our failures than our successes,* you shouldn't merely reflect on the statement; you should cite examples from your life, from the news, or from history. Essays filled with general, unsupported statements are not only unconvincing but also uninteresting.

Plagiarism

As you take notes, be aware that when you write your paper you must cite any sources you use, so record the information you'll need for parenthetical (in-text) citations. Consult a style guide for proper format of citations within the text of your paper and at the end (bibliography, works cited, references page). You'll be guilty of **plagiarism** if you don't properly give credit for words or ideas that you have taken from other writers.

Most people understand that they can't steal exact material (such as copying and pasting words or charts from a Web site), but some believe that paraphrasing other's words or ideas is acceptable. It isn't. Paraphrasing isn't just changing a few words in a sentence taken from another source. Unless the words or ideas are your own or they are considered general knowledge, you must cite the source of your information.

While you don't need to cite the source of well-known ideas such as evolution or easily accessible facts such as the date of the first moon landing, you *should* document less generally known ideas or opinions (for example, a news analyst's assessment of a Supreme Court decision), and less accessible facts (such as the number of motorcycles sold in the United States in a given year). Deciding what to cite can be a gray area, but play it safe. If you have doubts, cite the source.

Quoting and paraphrasing

When should you use quotations in a paper, and when should you paraphrase information instead? If you want to make a point about an author's language or style—as in the analysis of a literary work—use quotations. But don't quote an entire stanza if you are going to comment on only two words. And don't give up your responsibility to discuss a character simply by quoting a descriptive passage from a novel. Quoted material should support *your* ideas.

If you are concentrating on the information a source conveys rather than the author's expression, consider paraphrasing (putting the information in your own words) rather than quoting, especially if the passage is long and includes material you don't need. Ask yourself, "Why am I including this quotation?" If you have a good reason—an author's language, for example, or a particularly apt expression—go ahead. But often you only need the content or part of the information. Consider the following passage:

> Community-based policing has given rise to several important questions, among them the following: Should police officers address social problems that extend beyond particular crimes? Some experts on police reform say yes, while others say no. Although there is agreement that having police officers walk regular beats can decrease community suspicion and deter lawbreakers, the experts who are against greater involvement feel that giving police a broader responsibility by expecting them to deal with problems such as urban decay and irresponsible parenting is unrealistic and ultimately undesirable.

If you're writing about attitudes toward police reform, why not paraphrase the point that relates to your topic, as shown in the following paragraph?

Police-reform experts disagree about many issues, including whether or not police should involve themselves in social issues that go beyond their direct responsibility to deter crime and apprehend lawbreakers.

Don't pad a paper with quotations to add length (you'll irritate the instructor). And don't quote heavily to prove that you've read a source and have evidence for your points. Paraphrasing works just as well. Caution: Paraphrasing a source requires correct citation of the source of your ideas, just as a quotation does.

The Writing Assignment

Assignments vary widely, and you can use different strategies for each writing task. The main purpose of your project may be research, argument, analysis, or narrative. In each of these areas, you can learn some basic skills that will make the assignment easier. Step one is always the same: Make sure you understand the requirements of the assignment.

Research papers

A research paper is similar to other writing assignments. You should have a topic, thesis, introduction, good organization, unified and coherent paragraphs, transitions, and so on. A research paper should *not* consist of a series of quotations or footnoted facts loosely strung together.

Unlike other essays, a research paper depends on the use and citation of several sources of information, such as reference books, books related to your subject, relevant journal and magazine articles, speeches, and lectures. During the information-gathering stage, spend time in the library. Check electronic databases. Learn how to locate a variety of print and electronic materials that will give you a thorough (not one-sided) view of your topic. (See "Using the Internet for research," earlier in this chapter.) When you find information, take careful notes that include bibliographical information about your sources. Because practices for footnoting and preparing a bibliography vary, when you're assigned a research paper, ask your instructor to recommend a style guide.

Essays arguing a position from a single text

If your assignment is to write about a single text—for example, to take a position on an article in favor of regulating the Internet—read the text several times. Look up terms you're unsure of. Mark points that seem unclear or issues that may require research. Include outside research if allowed by the assignment. Be sure to cite material from other sources, just as you would in a research paper.

Identify the strongest and weakest arguments in the article. After analyzing the text, decide whether you agree or disagree with the author's position. When you write your paper, you should provide a fair summary of the position stated in the article, whether you're agreeing with it or not. In an argumentative essay you must support your own viewpoint *and* answer the opposition.

Essays analyzing a literary work

When you're asked to analyze a literary work, or one aspect of a literary work, stay close to the text. Your first job is to interpret meaning, which can take some time and several readings. Once you feel comfortable with your interpretation, take notes or mark the text to find support for your thesis. You'll use quotations from the work in your paper, so highlight those passages or lines that might be particularly effective.

Generally, when you write an essay on a nonliterary text, you focus on the content and the quality of the author's arguments. When you write about a literary text—a novel or a poem, for example—you must also pay close attention to the author's technique. In your notes, include specific words and images from the text, observations about structure (a poem's rhyme scheme, for example, or a novel's subplot), point of view, and tone. When you discuss features and techniques like these in your essay, you should relate them to a point you are making, usually about the author's theme or purpose.

Narrative, descriptive, and autobiographical essays

For some essays, you'll present your own thoughts, observations, and experiences, without reference to a text. As with essays that argue, explain, persuade, critique, inform, or analyze, you will need to gather information to develop your main ideas.

Before beginning an essay describing your Aunt Arlene for example, write down all the details you can about her, including any anecdotes that reveal her characteristics. At this point, you are gathering information, so don't worry about organizing your observations. If you haven't yet written a sentence stating a main idea, try to do so now. (For example, *Although Aunt Arlene prides herself on being no trouble to anyone, she finds ways to get everyone in the family to do what she wants.* Or *Aunt Arlene looks like a little old lady, but she acts like a teenager.*) Without a controlling theme, your essay will be a list of details with nothing to unify them or give them purpose. Eliminate information that does not relate to the central idea, which stems from the purpose of the writing.

When a college application asks for an autobiographical essay, your purpose will be to describe the traits, experiences, interests, achievements, and goals that show you're a good candidate for college admission. First, take notes about yourself, including things that emphasize your individuality. Later, you may decide not to include the no-hit softball game you pitched when you were nine, or every fast-food job you've ever had. But by making a complete list, you can look for patterns that will help you organize the content of the essay. When it's time to put your points in order, throw out unnecessary details, consolidate, and summarize. For example, you could mention that you held five fast-food jobs (but not specify each employer) while attending high school and becoming class valedictorian.

Chapter Check-Out

Questions

1. Determine whether the following passages should be quoted or paraphrased.

   a. "It was the best of times; it was the worst of times." (Dickens 1).

   b. "Dr. Kamdibe knew that he was close to his discovery in early February. By the following April, even the media had been alerted to the revolutionary work his lab was conducting. Finally, in June, the cure was announced." (Smith 32).

   c. "Shall I compare thee to a summer's day?" (Shakespeare 18).

2. Identify which of the following statements are true or false about writing:

   a. You will use all of the material you find when you do research for a writing assignment.

   b. You do not have to cite new information that you find in a current magazine or Web site.

   c. When in doubt, it is better to cite your sources.

   d. You should use paraphrasing to summarize long passages in your essays.

   e. Numerous long quotations are necessary in good essays.

   f. Preparing a detailed outline before you begin writing will help keep your writing focused and save time when you write a first draft.

g. If you find statistics on someone's Web blog, you can assume the information is current and accurate.

h. When you are writing an essay that analyzes a short story, you should focus more on the author's writing technique than on the story's content or plot.

Answers

1. a. quote; **b.** paraphrase; **c.** quote

2. a. false; **b.** false; **c.** true; **d.** true; **e.** false; **f.** true; **g.** false; **h.** true

Chapter 14

WRITING: FROM INTRODUCTION TO CONCLUSION

Chapter Check-In

❏ Develop a logical, organized outline

❏ Draft an interesting introduction

❏ Create cohesive paragraphs

❏ Write a powerful conclusion

A common misconception about writing is that the first draft must be perfect. A first draft is rarely a final draft. Even the best writers create multiple drafts before they are satisfied with their writing. In the first draft, you should focus on the introduction, connecting ideas within paragraphs, and the conclusion. No matter what the topic is, you want to have a strong opening and closing.

A good introduction catches the reader's attention and provides an overview to the topic. You can interest the reader from the start by using quotations or stories, posing a question, or stating an opinion or interesting fact. Paragraphs develop a single idea in a series of connected sentences. A unified paragraph stays focused on a single idea and is coherent and well developed. Your final statement should bring all of your points to a logical conclusion.

Working from a Thesis Statement

The first thing to look at when you're organizing your paper is the main idea, often called a thesis statement. Put yourself in the reader's place. Imagine how you would expect to see the central idea developed. Next, look at the notes you've taken. If you used your thesis statement as a guide in gathering information, you should see a pattern.

Look at the following thesis statement.

> Imposing sanctions on China would be a mistake because it would hurt the American economy, because sanctions are notoriously unsuccessful as a way to force change, and because the United States should not interfere in the internal policies of other countries.

This statement suggests that the paper will be divided into three main parts; it even indicates an order for where those sections will appear in the paper. When you go through your notes, decide where each note logically fits. For example, statistics about U.S. clothing manufacturers' increasing use of Chinese labor would fit into section one, and a note about the failure of sanctions in the Middle East would fit into section two.

Your thesis statement might not be this precise; or the kind of essay you're writing might not lend itself to such an obvious division. But from the moment you select a topic and decide on a thesis, you should be thinking about ways to develop it. This thinking leads to your organizing principle.

Let's review some common ways to organize writing. After you begin to write, you may change your mind because the process of writing often generates new ideas or suggests a different direction. Be flexible.

Spatial or chronological organization

Some topics lend themselves to organization based on **space or time.** A descriptive essay might work well if you begin with a distant view and move in closer. First, describe how an old wooden barn looks from the road, for example; then describe what you see when you stand directly in front of the barn. Next, describe the view (and the smells and sounds) when standing inside the barn door, and complete your description with what you see when you climb the ladder into the loft.

In the narration of an event and in some kinds of technical writing—describing a process, for example—you write about events in the order they occur. If you were writing about making a ceramic vase, you could divide the process into three stages: selecting and preparing the clay, forming and refining the shape of the vase on the potter's wheel, and glazing the piece and firing it in a kiln. The detailed steps in making the vase could then be organized sequentially (chronologically) in these sections.

Dividing a subject into categories

Just as you can divide a process into stages, you can divide a subject into **categories.** As you look over your notes, use your thesis statement as a guide and see if logical groupings emerge. Look at the following topic and thesis statement from a fictional student.

> TOPIC Write a paper addressing an environmental concern and suggesting ideas for a solution.
>
> THESIS The United States is losing its forests, and the solution is everyone's responsibility.

Note that the second half of this thesis statement is weak: *the solution is everyone's responsibility* is a vague assertion.

In looking over his research notes, the student quickly identifies the information that relates to the first part of the thesis statement (*Less than 10 percent of U.S. old-growth forests remain, U.S. consumption of wood is up 30 percent since 1930,* and so on). However, when he looks at the rest of his notes, he finds he has everything from *Logging bans have been effective in many areas* to *Don't use disposable diapers* to *Agricultural waste can be effectively processed to make building materials that provide excellent insulation.*

At this point he decides to create categories. He finds that many notes are related to simple, everyday actions that can help reduce wood and paper consumption (*using cloth diapers instead of disposable diapers, sending email instead of paper memos, using cloth shopping bags instead of paper or plastic bags, recycling newspapers,* and so on). Other information he has found in his research covers alternatives for wood, such as *agricultural waste, engineered wood manufactured by the forest-products industry, the use of steel studs in construction rather than wooden ones, a method of wall forming called "rammed earth construction,"* and so on. Then he notices that several notes relate to government actions—such as *logging bans, wilderness designations,* and *Forest Service reforms.*

He decides to use three general classifications as a principle of organization:

I. Problem

II. Solutions

    A. Consumer actions

    B. Alternatives to wood

    C. Government regulations

He may decide to change the order of the classifications when he writes his paper, but for now he has a principle of organization.

If some notes don't fit into these classifications, this student may want to add another category, or add some subsections. For example, if several notes deal with actions by major conservation groups, he may want to add a division under *Solutions* called *Conservation group activities.* Or, if he finds information relating to disadvantages of wood alternatives, he may add some subtopics under B; for example, *price, stability, public perception.*

Dividing material into categories is one of the most basic forms of organization. Make sure the categories are appropriate to the purpose of your paper and that you have sufficient information under each one. Remember that you will have more information and notes from your research than will relate directly to your thesis. Just because you discovered some interesting data during your research doesn't mean you must include this information in your paper. (See Chapter 13, "How to Research and Organize Your Writing.")

Organizing essays of comparison

Sometimes students have problems comparing and contrasting two topics. After gathering information, they fail to focus on the similarities and differences. When your topic involves comparison, you can organize in either of two ways.

First, you can discuss each subject separately, and then include a section in which you draw comparisons and contrasts between the two. With this organization, if you were comparing and contrasting two poems, you would write first about one—covering, for example, theme, language, images, tone, and rhyme scheme—and then you would write about the other, covering the same areas. In a third section, you would make a series of statements comparing and contrasting major aspects of the two poems. If you use this method to organize a comparison essay, make sure the separate discussions of the poems are parallel. That is, for the second poem, address points in the same order you used for the first poem. In the third section of the paper, avoid simply repeating what you said in sections one and two.

A second way of organizing requires you to decide first which aspects of the poems you want to compare and contrast (theme, language, imagery, tone, and so on) and then to structure your essay according to these elements. For example, if you begin with theme, you state the themes of both poems and compare them. Next, you compare the language of the two poems, then the imagery, then the tone, and so on.

When you use the second type of organization, you focus on similarities and differences. Because of this you are less likely to include material that isn't pertinent, and you avoid repetition by eliminating a separate compare-and-contrast section.

These two types of organization can be combined. For example, you may want to discuss each poem's theme separately, and then move into a point-by-point comparison of the other aspects of the poem (language, imagery, tone, and so on).

Inductive and deductive patterns of organization

In a logical argument, the pattern in which you present specific evidence and then draw a general conclusion is called **inductive.** This term can also be used to describe a method of approaching the material, particularly in a persuasive essay or one presenting an argument. You are using this method in an essay even when you state the general conclusion *first* and present supporting evidence in successive paragraphs. In most essays, it's common to begin with the general conclusion as a thesis statement.

EVIDENCE The student action committee failed to achieve a quorum in all six of its last meetings.

During the past year, the student action committee has proposed four plans for changing the grievance procedure and has been unable to adopt any of them.

According to last month's poll in the student newspaper, 85 percent of the respondents had not heard of the student action committee.

Two openings on the committee have remained unfilled for eight months because no one has applied for membership.

CONCLUSION The student action committee is an ineffective voice for students at this university. [A general conclusion is drawn from specific evidence or examples. Note: In an essay, this would be a thesis statement.]

Another type of organization borrowed from logical argument is called **deductive.** With this pattern, you begin with a generalization and then apply it to specific instances. In a timed writing, you might be given a general statement such as *It's better to be safe than sorry* or *Beauty is in the eye of the beholder* and then asked to agree or disagree, providing examples that support your view.

With such essays, you aren't proving or disproving the truth of a statement, but offering an opinion and supporting it with examples. If you begin with a generalization such as *Beauty is in the eye of the beholder,* for example, you could cite instances such as different standards for human beauty in different cultures, or different views of beauty in architecture from era to era. You could also use examples from your own experience, such as your sister's fascination with desert landscapes in contrast to your boredom with them.

Connecting paragraphs in an essay

Your essay should move smoothly from paragraph to paragraph, each point growing out of the preceding one. If you are shifting directions or moving to a different point, prepare your reader with a transition. Use transitional phrases to guide the reader through your paper: *additionally, as a result, generally speaking, next, in contrast, on the other hand, similarly, at the same time, later,* or *in conclusion.* Achieving continuity throughout the essay is similar to achieving continuity in a paragraph.

Outlines

Creating an **outline,** either a formal or an informal one, helps you organize your research and create a logical flow to your writing. Sometimes an outline helps you see problems in the original plan, and you can eliminate them before you spend time writing.

If you prefer writing papers without an outline, try an experiment. Create an outline *after* a paper is finished to see if your organization is clear and logical. This exercise may convince you that outlining is helpful.

Informal outlines

An *informal outline* can be a simple list of main points. You can refine it by following each main point with notes about the evidence or examples that support it. You are grouping your notes. A simple outline like this is often all the organization you need. It is especially valuable for timed writings or essay exams. Thinking through your approach before you begin—and jotting down your thoughts—will help you avoid rambling and moving away from the assignment.

Formal outlines

Sometimes you may want to prepare a more *formal outline*. You may even be asked to submit an outline with a writing assignment. Here are a few tips for creating outlines.

Use Roman numerals (I., II., V.) for main topics in your outline. Beneath each of the main topics, use capital letters (A., B., C.) to list the information supporting each of the main topics. Then list each subtopic using Arabic numbers (1., 2., 3.). If you have small details that support the subtopics, use lowercase letters (a., b., c.). Most word-processing programs have automatic outline features that will indent and align topics and subtopics for you.

I.

    A.

    B.

        1.

        2.

           a.

           b.

Make outline topics and subtopics parallel in structure. For example, if you use a complete sentence for the first topic, use complete sentences for all subsequent topics. If you use one word or a phrase for the first subtopic, use one word or a phrase for the following ones.

Watch the logic of your outline. The main topics generally indicate the basic structure of your essay. The second level of your outline (A., B., C., and so on) covers the major ideas that contribute to and support the larger units. The next level of subtopics is for narrower points related to these ideas. Don't include irrelevant ideas in your outline. Make sure each element logically fits under its heading.

Each topic and subtopic should have at least one related topic or subtopic. That is, you cannot have an I. without an II., or an A. without a B., and so on. Topics and subtopics are divisions of your subject, so you can't divide something into one part. If your outline shows single topics or subtopics, reevaluate to see whether you are misplacing or poorly stating your headings. Maybe the information should be worked into an existing larger category or divided into two topics or subtopics.

Sentence outlines and topic outlines

In a *sentence outline,* all elements are stated in complete sentences. In a *topic outline,* the elements may be presented as single words or as phrases. Study the following examples.

Sentence outline

I. Many high school classes do not prepare students for large university classes.

    A. Nontracked high school classes don't challenge more capable students to achieve at their highest level.

        1. Less competition leads some students to try to "get by" rather than excel.

        2. Inflated grading of good students in nontracked classes can lead to false expectations.

    B. High school classes are not designed to encourage individual responsibility, which is required in large university classes.

        1. Required attendance in high school may lead students to react to less rigid attendance requirements by cutting classes at the college level.

        2. High school teachers assign daily homework and reading assignments, whereas university professors generally make long-term assignments.

        3. High school teachers frequently spend more time with individual students than do professors in large universities.

II. Some high schools offer programs to help students prepare for university classes.

Topic outline

I. Lack of preparation of high school students for university classes

    A. Nontracked high school classes

        1. Less competition

        2. Inflated grades

    B. Less individual responsibility in high school classes

        1. Required attendance

        2. Homework and daily assignments

        3. Individual attention from teachers

II. Programs to prepare high school students for university classes

Getting Started

The first thing to remember when you begin to write is that the first draft does not need to be perfect. Count on rewriting. Your first draft may well be a mix of planning and improvising—taking you in a direction you hadn't originally intended. Even when you begin a first draft, you may make changes in your thesis statement or your organizational plan.

This guideline changes for timed writing assignments. You will probably have time for only one draft, so organization is crucial. Spend a few moments planning your answer, noting examples, and then begin writing.

Introductions

The opening paragraph or **introduction** of argumentative or analytical papers should indicate the purpose and establish the tone. The introduction does not need to be a certain length, although it should be well developed. (For timed writings, an introductory statement rather than a paragraph is sufficient.) The introduction should catch the attention of readers and provide context about the paper's topic. If you are discussing a particular book, article, or work of art, include its title and author in your opening paragraph. If you have trouble with introductions, try writing it after you have written the rest of your paper.

What to avoid

An introduction is important for setting the tone of your essay. There is no single right way to begin a paper, but here are some guidelines you should keep in mind:

- Avoid obvious statements or generalities.

    Drug use is an important issue in high schools today.

    Capital punishment is a very controversial subject.

- Avoid weak or thinly veiled restatements of the assignment.

    It is illuminating to trace the clothing imagery in *King Lear*.

    A person can make many interesting points in comparing the poems "The Happy Meercat" and "To a Wolf."

- Avoid flat statements of the thesis or main idea, particularly using *I* or *this essay.*

    In this paper I will show that the overemphasis on winning is dangerous for young athletes.

    This essay will cover the many opportunities available to young people who choose computer science as a major.

- Avoid defining a term that doesn't need defining or that leads the reader nowhere.

    The novel *Silas Marner* by George Eliot is about a man who is a miser. What is a miser? According to the definition in *Webster's New World Dictionary,* a miser is "a greedy, stingy person who hoards money for its own sake."

Suggestions for introductions

An introduction should lead naturally into the rest of your paper and must be appropriate to its purpose, topic, and tone. Here are some suggestions for openings; but use judgment in applying them, and be careful not to overuse these techniques. Although beginning with an anecdote can be effective for some papers, don't force one where it doesn't belong. A story about your indecisive father is not the best way to begin a paper analyzing the character of *Hamlet.*

- Use a relevant quotation from the work you are discussing.

    "I am encompassed by a wall, high and hard and stone, with only my brainy nails to tear it down. And I cannot do it." Kerewin Holmes, one of the main characters in Keri Hulme's novel *The Bone People,* describes herself as both physically and emotionally alone in a tower she has built by the New Zealand Sea. Throughout the novel Hulme uses images—the tower, muteness, physical beatings, the ocean—to suggest her characters' isolation from each other and the community around them.

- Provide background or context for your thesis statement.

    Until the second half of this century, Americans spent the country's natural resources freely. They mined for minerals, diverted rivers, and replaced wilderness with cities and towns. In the process they cut down forests that had been in place for thousands of years. Now, the reality that progress has its price is obvious to almost everyone. Only 10 percent of old-growth forests in the

United States remain intact, with demand for wood products expected to grow by 50 percent in the next fifty years. The country is in danger of losing its forests altogether unless citizens pursue solutions that range from everyday recycling to using wood alternatives to actively supporting government regulations.

■ Ask a question that leads to your thesis statement.

Is the United States still a country where the middle class thrives? Strong evidence suggests that the traditional American view of a successful middle class is fading. At the very least, the prospects for someone who stands in the economic middle have significantly changed since the 1980s. Years ago middle-class people expected to own their own homes in the suburbs and send their children to college. Today, for many people, these expectations have become distant dreams. Three factors—growing unemployment, wage disparity in the labor force, and rising costs for education and goods—suggest that the middle class may be shrinking.

■ Begin with a relevant anecdote that leads to the thesis statement.

Doug was the star in my high school senior class. He was captain of the football team, dated the prettiest girls, charmed his teachers, and managed to get A's and B's seemingly without studying. When he headed off to a big Midwestern university, we weren't surprised. But when he was home again a year later on academic probation, many of us wondered what happened. Doug told me candidly that his year at the university was far removed from anything he'd experienced in high school. His small, noncompetitive high school classes hadn't prepared him for a large university where the professors didn't know his name, let alone his role as a big man on campus. I believe programs to help students like Doug make the transition from high school to college could help reduce the high failure rate among college freshmen.

■ Speak to your readers, and ask them to imagine themselves in a situation you create.

Imagine being escorted into a room and asked to disrobe every time you want to take an airplane trip. Picture someone in a uniform grilling you about your background or even hooking you up to a lie detector machine. Such scenarios seem impossible in America, but experts agree that the U.S. may be forced to take extreme measures to combat the increasing threat of domestic terrorism.

Your topic may suggest any number of creative beginnings. Try to go beyond the obvious in your opening sentences. For example, which of the following two openings for an essay on the qualities of a good mate sounds more interesting?

> STUDENT 1 It is important to look for many qualities in the person you choose to spend your life with.

> STUDENT 2 Finding a mate is hard enough. Finding a mate you're happy with for many years may seem nearly impossible.

Paragraphs

A **paragraph** develops one idea with a series of logically connected sentences. Most paragraphs function as small essays, each with a main topic and several related sentences that support it.

How many paragraphs do you need in your paper? That depends on what you have to say. The idea that an essay should consist of five paragraphs—an introduction, three paragraphs of examples, and a conclusion—is too rigid, although some students are taught to organize information in this way. You may have more than three examples or points to make, and you may have an example or point that requires several paragraphs to develop. Don't limit yourself. Let the topic and supporting points guide you in creating logical, cohesive paragraphs.

Paragraph length

Paragraphs can vary in length. For example, short paragraphs are used in newspaper stories where the emphasis is on reporting information without discussion, or in technical writing where the emphasis is on presenting facts such as statistics and measurements without analysis. Written dialogue also consists of short paragraphs, with a new paragraph for each change of speaker. In an essay, a short paragraph can also be effectively used for dramatic effect or transition.

> But the reconciliation was never to take place. Her grandmother died as Jillian was driving home from the airport.

Generally, you should avoid a series of extremely short paragraphs in your essays. They suggest poor development of an idea.

On the other hand, paragraphs that are a page or more in length are difficult for most readers, who like to see a subject divided into shorter sections. Examine long paragraphs to see whether you have gone beyond covering one idea or if you are guilty of repetition, wordiness, or rambling. But don't arbitrarily split a long paragraph. Make sure each paragraph meets the requirement of a single main idea with sentences that support it.

Paragraph unity

A **unified paragraph** is one that focuses on only one idea. Look at the following example of a paragraph that *lacks* unity.

> Identification of particular genes can lead to better medicine. For example, recently scientists identified a defective gene that appears to cause hemochromatosis, or iron overload. Iron overload is fairly easily cured if it is recognized and treated early, but currently it is often misdiagnosed because it mimics more familiar conditions. The problem is that when not treated in time, iron overload leads to a variety of diseases, from diabetes to liver cancer. The identification of the faulty gene can prevent misdiagnosis by allowing physicians, through a screening test, to identify patients who carry it and treat them before the condition becomes too advanced. *It is interesting that most people don't realize the exact role of iron in the body.* They know that it is important for their health, but few are aware that only about 10 percent of the iron in food is normally absorbed by the small intestine. Most of the rest is tied up in hemoglobin, which carries oxygen from the lungs.

The first sentence of the paragraph presents the main idea that identification of genes leads to improved medical care. This idea is developed by the example of how the identification of a gene causing iron overload can lead to better diagnosis and early treatment. However, in the italicized sentence, the paragraph begins to wander. It is a topic sentence for a different paragraph, one about the role of iron in the body, and not about a benefit of genetic research.

Sometimes a sentence or two buried in the middle of a paragraph can break the unity of the paragraph, as in this example.

> Moving out of my parents' house and into an apartment didn't bring me the uncomplicated joy that I had expected. First of all, I had to struggle to pay the rent every month, and the landlord was much less understanding than my parents. Then I realized I had to do my own laundry, clean up the place now and then, and fix my own meals. *One nice thing about my mother is that she is an excellent cook. She even attended a French cooking school before she married my father.* It's true that I liked the greater freedom I had in my apartment—no one

constantly asking me what time I'd be home, no one nagging me about cleaning up my room or raking the front lawn—but I wasn't thrilled with spending most of a Saturday getting rid of a cockroach infestation, or doing three loads of smelly laundry on a Sunday night.

Notice how the italicized sentences interrupt the flow of the paragraph, which is really about the down side of leaving home and not about the writer's mother and her cooking skills.

To test the unity of your paragraphs, locate the topic sentence (the clear statement of the paragraph's central idea) and then test the other sentences to see if they develop that particular idea or if they wander off in another direction.

Paragraph coherence

Along with developing a single idea, a paragraph should be well organized. You can use many of the same principles—chronology, inductive and deductive patterns, and so on—that you use to organize complete essays.

Once you've decided on the order of your details, make sure the connections between sentences in the paragraph are clear. The smooth, logical flow of sentences within a paragraph is called **paragraph coherence.** Write each sentence with the previous one in mind.

Connecting sentences through ideas

Connect your sentences through their content, by picking up something from one sentence and carrying it into the next.

Follow a sentence that makes a general point with a specific, clear illustration of that point. Look at the following example.

> The gap in pay between people with basic skills and people without them seems to be widening. In one comparison, the pay difference between women of varied mathematical skills had grown from $.93 an hour in 1978 to $1.71 an hour in 1986.

Here, the second sentence is a clear illustration of the point made in the first sentence. But look at how coherence can be lost in a paragraph, as in the following example.

> The gap in pay between people with basic skills and people without them seems to be widening. Women are now playing a more important role in the work force than they have since World War II, when

many had to fill the positions of men who were overseas. The pay difference between women of varied mathematical skills has grown considerably, from \$.93 an hour in 1978 to \$1.71 an hour in 1986.

In this example, the second sentence is not clearly connected to the first. Sentence three returns to the subject, but the continuity of the idea has been weakened.

You can also use one sentence to reflect or comment on the previous sentence, as in the following example.

The idea that in America hard work leads to financial success has been one of our most successful exports. For decades immigrants have arrived on American soil with a dream that here they can have what was impossible in their home countries, where they were limited by class structure or few opportunities.

As you review your paragraphs, be sure that such reflections logically follow from the previous statement. In the preceding paragraph, the idea about immigrants arriving on American soil with the preconceived notion that they will succeed is tied to the point in the first sentence that the American dream has been a successful export.

You can also connect sentences by asking a question and following it with an answer or making a statement and following it with a question.

Why should the government invest in research? Research leads to technological advances that create employment, as was shown in the years following World War II.

Polls indicate that many Americans favor regulation of the Internet. Are they willing to pay both with their tax dollars and their freedoms?

The sentences in these two examples are linked by words as well as by ideas. In the first example, the word *research* has been picked up from the question and repeated in the answer. In the second example, the pronoun *they* in the question has its antecedent (*Americans*) in the previous statement. Be careful not to overuse the question technique, or you risk a negative reaction from readers.

Connecting with words and phrases

One way to achieve paragraph coherence is by connecting ideas. As shown in the last two examples, words and phrases can help strengthen the connection between sentences.

- Use a pronoun whose antecedent appears in the previous sentence.

  Gabriel Garcia Marquez suspends the laws of reality in his novels. *He* creates bizarre and even magical situations that reveal character in surprising ways.

- Repeat a key word or phrase.

  The idea of a perfect society, though never realized, continues to intrigue political *philosophers*. None of *these philosophers* seem to agree on where perfection lies.

- Use a synonym.

  According to my research, *physical beauty is* considered a more important asset for women than for men. *Looks* are everything, according to several girls I spoke to, while the boys I interviewed believed their athletic abilities and social status were at least as important as their appearance.

- Use word patterns, such as *first, second, third,* and so on.

  The reasons the dean announced her decision today are clear. *First,* students will recognize that she is listening to their concerns. *Second,* faculty will applaud the end of a disruptive period of indecision. *Third,* wealthy alumni—though not particularly pleased by the plan—will be happy that the controversy will be off the front page of the paper.

- Use transitional words and phrases. Many words and phrases signal connections between sentences in a paragraph or between paragraphs in a paper. Look at the italicized words below.

  The main character worships her. *Later,* his adoration changes to hatred.

  The church stood at the top of the hill. *Below* stretched miles of orchards.

  She treated him well. *For example,* she bought him a car and new clothes.

  The product promised to grow new hair. *But* all he grew was a rash.

  Hamlet disdained Ophelia. *As a result,* she killed herself.

  Elizabeth was angry at Travis. *In fact,* she wanted nothing to do with him.

The plan is too expensive. *Furthermore,* it won't work.

No one volunteered to help. *In other words,* no one cared.

In the preceding examples, the italicized words or phrases clearly connect the second sentence to the first by creating a particular relationship. Vary the transitional words you use.

Following is a list of transitional words and phrases classified according to the relationships they suggest. These words and phrases, when used appropriately, can help you connect ideas in your writing.

Time or place: *above, across from, adjacent to, afterward, before, behind, below, beyond, earlier, elsewhere, farther on, here, in the distance, near by, next to, opposite to, to the left, to the right*

Example: *for example, for instance, specifically, to be specific*

Contrast: *but, however, nevertheless, on the contrary, on the other hand*

Similarity: *similarly, in the same way, equally important*

Consequence: *accordingly, as a result, consequently, therefore*

Emphasis: *indeed, in fact, of course*

Amplification: *and, again, also, further, furthermore, in addition, moreover, too*

Restatement: *in other words, more simply stated, that is, to clarify*

Summary and conclusion: *altogether, finally, in conclusion, in short, to summarize*

Conclusions

Knowing when and how to end your paper can be difficult. Writing a strong **conclusion** is like tying a ribbon around a gift package. It's the last thing you do, but it also gives your paper a finishing touch. If the ending is powerful and effective, your reader will feel satisfied.

What to avoid

Before you can write a strong conclusion, you should know what to avoid. Here are some common errors.

■ Don't introduce a new topic that has not been discussed in your paper. For example, if your essay has been about the loss of forests and possible solutions for the high consumption of wood products, don't end with a paragraph about a different environmental issue, such as the disappearance of the California condor.

■ Don't trail off with a weak statement or a statement that leaves your reader up in the air.

> The Internet, free of regulation, has opened a world of information and ideas to everyone. Children enjoy learning on the computer.

■ Don't simply repeat your thesis or main idea in the same words.

> As stated earlier, clothing imagery shows the changes in *King Lear* throughout the play.

■ Don't apologize for or suggest doubts about your thesis.

> For a variety of reasons, middle-class expectations today differ from those in the 1980s. It is possible, however, that the difference is not particularly illuminating about life in the United States.

In a short paper (less than five pages, for example), you may use a brief concluding sentence instead of a formal conclusion. Formal conclusions can sometimes be superfluous, particularly if the conclusion is a long summary of what he or she just read. Instead, end your paper with a strong final sentence.

Suggestions for conclusions

A strong conclusion should tie up the loose ends of your essay, refer to the central theme (thesis), give your readers a sense of completion, and leave them with a strong impression. You can do this with a single statement or with a paragraph. If you write a concluding paragraph, consider the following possibilities.

■ End with an appropriate quotation. Notice in the following example how the writer also pulls together loose ends and briefly refers to the thesis.

> Throughout the novel the characters suffer both from their isolation and from their attempts to end it. Kerewin burns her tower, Joe beats his son and goes to prison, and Simon—who barely

survives the beating—must painfully find his way back to those he loves. Recurring images dramatize their journeys, which end in a reconciliation between being alone and being part of a community. Kerewin describes the home that will now take the place of her lonely tower: "I decided on a shell-shape, a regular spiral of rooms expanding around the decapitated Tower . . . privacy, apartness, but all connected and all part of the whole."

■ Without repeating your thesis word for word, you can unify your essay by relating the final paragraph to a point in the introduction.

Preserving old-growth forests and finding substitutes for wood should concern everyone who cares about the environment. The days when Americans could view this country as an unlimited provider of resources are as gone as roaming herds of buffalo and pioneers in covered wagons.

■ End with a story related to your thesis.

On a recent trip to the airport, I stood at the ticket counter behind an angry woman. It seems she'd forgotten her photo ID, and the attendant told her she couldn't fly without it. After calling the clerk a storm trooper and threatening to sue the airline, the woman turned to me and said, "You tell me. Do I *look* like the kind of person who would blow up a plane?" I didn't answer, but I wondered how in the future this woman would react to a fifteen-minute interview about herself or to a uniformed attendant patting her down.

■ Another way to conclude a paper is to summarize the main points. But because summaries aren't particularly interesting conclusions, consider using this technique only if your paper is fairly long and if a summary would be helpful to your reader. Keep the summary brief, and avoid indecisive or overly general final sentences, such as *For all these reasons, the Internet should not be regulated.*

Chapter Check-Out

Questions

1. Evaluate the following introductions as effective or ineffective.
   a. "You live by the sword; you die by the sword."
   b. In this essay I will prove smoking is dangerous.
   c. Who are the homeless in America?
   d. Homelessness is a big problem.

2. Evaluate the following concluding sentences as effective or ineffective.
   a. Although not all of my conclusions are supportable, I still think this law is dangerous.
   b. As explained above, global warming is a serious concern for everyone on the planet.
   c. For all these reasons, my position is correct.

3. Indicate whether the following statements about paragraphs are true or false.
   a. Paragraphs should be divided based on the ideas they contain.
   b. Paragraphs should always be five sentences long.
   c. Paragraphs have unity if they are focused on a single idea.
   d. A word or phrase can be a unifying focus for an entire paragraph.

Answers

1. a. effective; b. ineffective; c. effective; d. ineffective

2. a. ineffective; b. ineffective; c. ineffective

3. a. true; b. false; c. true; d. true

Chapter 15

REVISING AND EDITING

Chapter Check-In

❏ Create an engaging title

❏ Review your first draft

❏ Edit to correct grammar and mechanics

❏ Use a revision checklist to prepare a final draft

Once you have written a solid first draft of your essay or paper, you can begin refining, revising, editing, and polishing your writing. At this point, you may think of a title that captures the essence of your topic and theme.

After the first review is completed, edit and revise the essay. You may find it helpful to read your draft aloud, or ask someone you trust to review your essay. Editing involves looking at the grammatical and mechanical content of your work. Revising means not only looking at grammar but also the overall effect of the essay. Editing and revising ensure that the final draft fits the assignment and audience, is grammatically and mechanically correct, and is well organized and supported.

Titles

While you're writing an essay, if you have an idea for a title, write it down. Often the best time to choose a title is after you've completed a first draft and read it over. Be creative with your title, but don't overdo it. For example, if you're writing a paper about deforestation, titling it "Knock on Wood" might seem clever at first, but it doesn't accurately fit the topic. (Titles are not required for all types of writing—timed essays, for example. Check your assignment.)

Use good judgment when choosing a title. Consider the formality and tone of your essay and your audience. "No More Mr. Nice Guy" might be a good title for a personal essay on the loss of your gullibility, but you should think twice before using it as the title of an analytical paper on Shakespeare's character Macbeth.

The best advice is to strike a balance: Avoid the overly general and dull, or the too clever and obscure. When choosing a title, consider using a quotation from a work you are writing about, an effective phrase from your own essay, or an appropriate figure of speech.

"Sleep No More": The Role of Macbeth's Conscience
RATHER THAN Macbeth's Conscience

"I'm Nobody": Finding Emily Dickinson in Her Poetry
RATHER THAN Emily Dickinson and Her Poetry

Gaining Safety or Losing Freedom: The Debate over Airport Security Measures
RATHER THAN Airport Security Measures

Only Skin Deep?
RATHER THAN The Importance of Beauty to Today's Woman

Fit to Be Tried: An Examination of the McNaughton Rule
RATHER THAN Judging Legal Sanity

Reviewing the First Draft

You will probably make your most extensive revisions as you read your first draft. Here are a few suggestions that can help you in reviewing the first draft.

- If possible, allow some time between writing the first draft and reviewing it, so you can look at your first draft with fresh eyes.

- Try reading your paper aloud to yourself. Sometimes your ear catches problems and errors your eye misses.

- Ask someone you trust to read your draft and offer suggestions. And remember: You are looking for an honest, objective opinion, not praise. Evaluate your reader's suggestions carefully, and decide for yourself whether or not to act on them.

■ Remember that nothing is unchangeable. Until preparation of your final draft, you can change your paper's thesis, organization, emphasis, tone, and so on. A review of your first draft should *not* be limited to minor mechanical errors.

■ Use a revision checklist to make sure you've reviewed your draft thoroughly. The checklists later in this chapter will be especially helpful as you review your first draft.

Preparing the Final Draft

You may be able to move directly from your revised first draft to a final draft, but careful writers often prepare several drafts before they are satisfied with a piece. As you rewrite, you may continue to discover wordy constructions, poor connections, awkward sentences, and other issues.

Writing and editing a draft

While you can quickly handwrite research notes or an outline for your paper, you may want to use a computer to produce a first draft that's legible and easy to edit. You can do much of your editing directly on the screen. If you think of a better way to say what you've just said, make the change immediately and move on. For more global editing, however, many writers like to print out sections or complete drafts, mark them up by hand, and then go back to the computer to input the changes. This method has advantages. Working on the screen limits you to a small section of text. Scrolling up and down in a long, complex document can be confusing. Another advantage of printing out your essay is that it forces you to slow down and read carefully. Because most of us can type quickly on a computer, our fingers may get ahead of our thoughts. Remember that good writing requires deliberation, evaluation, and judgment.

Spell-check, grammar-check, and search-and-replace functions

A *spell-check* function is useful for catching misspelled words, typos, and accidental repetitions (*the the*). But the spell-checker won't flag a word that is actually a word, even if it isn't the one you intended—for example, if you inadvertently type *form* for *from*. Spell-checking also doesn't distinguish between words that sound alike but are spelled differently and have different meanings (*it's/its, here/hear, their/they're/there*). Use the spell-checker as an aid, not as a replacement for your own careful proofreading.

Grammar- or style-checkers require even more caution, because grammar and style are less clear-cut than spelling. Many writers don't use these functions at all, and unless you already have a good grasp of grammar, these functions can be misleading. For example, grammar-checkers may catch pronoun agreement and reference errors, but not dangling participles or faulty parallelism. Some grammar-checkers flag possible usage problems and passive constructions, but they also flag every sentence beginning with a conjunction (*for, and, nor, but, or, yet, so*). The checker may also flag contractions and every sentence ending with a preposition—"errors" that current usage permits. If you use your computer's grammar-check function, do so critically.

A *search-and-replace* function lets you correct a particular error throughout your paper automatically. However, use caution with the Replace All command, or you could replace one error with another. It's a good idea to evaluate every instance of a misspelled word rather than using the automatic, Replace All command.

Final draft and layout

You can use your computer's word-processing and layout functions to produce a professional-looking final draft. If you are doing an assignment for a course, be sure to check with the instructor regarding the format requirements for your paper. For example, your instructor may require the following format: Times New Roman 12-point type, double-spaced text, 1-inch margins, a title page, inserted page numbers, and running heads. The computer's page-layout functions can help you create a properly formatted paper that meets specific requirements—MLA and APA style, for example.

If it's appropriate, you can present some information in tables, charts, or graphs, and you can import graphics. Be careful not to overdo graphics, varied type fonts, colors, design elements, and formatting. Don't confuse a good-looking paper with a well-written one. Although some readers may be initially impressed with a document that looks nice, special formatting and design features can't compensate for poorly expressed ideas. Many readers are distracted by too much formatting—boldface, italic type, bullets, and similar elements.

Checklists for Improving Your First Draft

A good first draft can almost always be improved by revision, editing, and rewriting. As you learn to evaluate your own writing more critically, you will be able to improve it. The following checklists will help guide you from a good first draft to an improved, refined final draft.

Purpose, audience, and tone

These elements deal with the overall effect of your essay and should guide you throughout your writing. Ask yourself the following questions:

✓ If I am writing in response to an assignment, does my essay fulfill all the required elements of the assignment?

✓ Is my topic too broad or too general?

✓ Do I state my thesis or main idea early in the paper? If I don't state a thesis or main idea, is it clearly implied so there can be no mistake about the purpose of my paper?

✓ Is my thesis or main idea interesting and compelling? If this is an essay of argument, is my thesis statement fair? Do I address opposing viewpoints?

✓ Is my tone appropriate to my audience and purpose? Does my audience have any special requirements?

✓ Is my tone consistent throughout the essay?

Examples, evidence, and details

These are specific details in the writing process. When you read your essay, you can determine whether you have used these elements well by considering the following questions:

✓ Have I adequately developed my thesis or main idea? Do I use specific details rather than generalities?

✓ Are my examples and evidence accurate, relevant, and convincing?

✓ Do I use quotations appropriately? Is too much of my paper quoted from other sources? Do I paraphrase carefully?

✓ Do I correctly cite sources for the words and ideas of others?

Structure

Use an outline to determine the structure of your paper, but be aware that you may need to alter it as you write. Keep in mind the following points:

✓ Do I have a principle of organization? Do I avoid repetition and digression?

✓ Is the organization of my writing appropriate to my topic and thesis?

✓ Does my introduction catch the reader's attention; does my conclusion summarize and tie up the loose ends of my paper?

✓ Are my paragraphs well developed, unified, and coherent?

✓ Does one paragraph flow into the next? Do I use transitions between paragraphs?

✓ Are my examples, evidence, and details in the best order? Do I save the strongest point for last?

Language and style

Use a dictionary and thesaurus or your computer's word-processing tools to help with language and style. Ask yourself the following questions:

✓ Have I chosen my words carefully? Am I sure of meanings?

✓ Is my language appropriate to my purpose, tone, and audience?

✓ Have I avoided wordy expressions, slang, and clichés?

✓ Have I avoided jargon and pretentious language?

✓ Have I used idioms correctly?

✓ Have I followed the guidelines of current English usage?

✓ Have I avoided sexism in the use of nouns and pronouns?

✓ Have I chosen the active over the passive voice in sentence structure?

Sentence construction

Use your editing and revision skills to make sure your sentences are well constructed. Keep the following points in mind:

✓ Are my sentences correct? Have I avoided fragments and run-ons?

✓ Are my modifiers in the right place? Do I have any dangling modifiers?

✓ Do my subjects and predicates agree in number?

✓ Do I keep constructions parallel?

✓ Have I avoided short, choppy sentences?

✓ Do I combine sentences effectively?

✓ Do I avoid monotony by varying my sentences in length and structure?

Grammar

Use this book to augment your grammar skills and keep in mind the following points:

✓ Have I checked

spelling (including correct plural forms, hyphenation)

capitalization

correct use and consistency of verb tenses

agreement (nouns, verbs, pronouns)

pronoun cases

pronoun antecedents

use of adjectives with linking verbs

comparative degrees of adjectives and adverbs

✓ Does my punctuation make my meaning clear? Have I followed punctuation rules?

Commas with nonrestrictive elements; no commas with restrictive elements

Commas with interrupting elements; with introductory phrases and clauses when necessary; between series items; between independent clauses

Correct use of periods and question marks

Correct use (and not overuse) of exclamation marks

Correct use of semicolons and colons

Correct use (and not overuse) of dashes and parentheses

Correct use (and not overuse) of quotation marks

Correct use of other punctuation with quotation marks

Chapter Check-Out

Questions

1. Evaluate the following essay titles as effective or ineffective.

   a. Capital Punishment

   b. Skiing Vail: Tips for the Best Vacation on the Slopes

   c. The World of Entomology: Bugs

   d. "Lord of the Rings": Translating J.R.R. Tolkien's Novels into Movies

2. Identify whether the following steps in the writing process should be done in the (first draft) or in the (final draft) stage.

   a. Writing a conclusion

   b. Creating a title

   c. Writing an introduction

   d. Checking spelling and usage

3. True or false: The writer should ask the following questions at the revision stage.

   a. Does my writing fit the assignment?

   b. Have I considered the audience?

   c. Do I use transitions between and within paragraphs?

   d. Have I checked spelling and grammar?

Answers

1. **a.** ineffective; **b.** effective; **c.** ineffective; **d.** effective

2. **a.** first draft; **b.** final draft; **c.** first draft; **d.** final draft

3. **a.** true; **b.** true; **c.** true; **d.** true

REVIEW QUESTIONS

Use these Review Questions to practice what you've learned in this book and to build your confidence in the grammar, usage, and style skills necessary for good writing. After you work through the review questions, the problem-solving exercises, and the fun and useful practice projects, you will be on your way to achieving your goal of writing well. For more quiz questions related to this book, go to our Web site: www.cliffsnotes.com.

QUESTIONS

Chapters 1–5

1. Identify the part of speech of the underlined word(s) in the following sentences.

    a. Jessica and Tony plan to visit <u>Ireland</u> again this year.

    b. Will his mother go with <u>them</u> this time?

    c. The daisies are a <u>little</u> wilted, but they are still pretty.

    d. She went <u>reluctantly</u> to the gym.

    e. We found a photo of our grandparents <u>under</u> a box of books in the attic.

    f. Arriving before the others, Corry was <u>eager</u> to get to work.

Chapters 6 and 7

2. Identify the common sentence errors in the following sentences. If there are no errors, write **No Error** in the blank.

    a. Although he had excellent test scores, Stan did not think his application was impressive since he had not participated in any extracurricular activities._____

    b. I am waiting for the bus it started to rain._____

    c. The hushed colors and heavier textures of Nicholas Razinski in his later years, often called his darker or more mature period._____

    d. In order to book our trip to Moscow, we had to wait for the agent and have patience._____

Chapters 8–10

3. Fill in the blank: Add correct punctuation to the following sentences. If no punctuation is needed, write **NP** in the blank.

    a. I have labeled all the plants by kingdom and phylum_____ This will aid us in the following areas _____ research _____ review_____ and _____ presentation of our science project_____

    b. Does she know_____ although it does not really matter_____ about the reward for the lost child_____

    c. "Stop_____ " she exclaimed in terror_____

    d. "This product is flammable _____" Erik read aloud_____

Chapter 11

4. Choose the correct word in the following sentences.

    a. The market correction should not <u>effect/affect</u> home sales in the year ahead.

    b. <u>Beside/Besides</u>, I am getting a new computer next month.

    c. <u>It's/Its</u> not quite as cold as the report predicted.

    d. The diversity of <u>it's/its</u> students was a strength of the program.

    e. <u>Lay/Lie</u> your glasses where you can see them.

    f. My cat, Minka, <u>lays/lies</u> at the foot of the bed each night.

    g. He spotted <u>there/their/they're</u> mistake immediately.

    h. <u>There/Their/They're</u> the best friends we have in town.

5. Identify which of the following sentences are wordy and which sentences are correct as written.

    a. Being the woman in the front office, Carol was often accustomed to frequent intrusions.

    b. We stayed until after the conclusion of the movie to see the credits at the end.

    c. Although the rain never relented, Claire played in the tennis tournament all day.

Chapters 12 and 13

6. Identify the following as a topic or a thesis.

   a. The Luddite movement in England had a tremendous impact on labor relations.

   b. Marxism is popular in Eastern European universities.

   c. Dante Gabriel Rossetti was a poet and painter.

   d. Origami is a beautiful art form that requires simplicity and precision.

Chapters 14 and 15

7. Identify whether the following statements about writing are true or false.

   a. Writers should cite all information and ideas they take from another source—both print and electronic.

   b. Introductions should never state the thesis main ideas directly.

   c. Start a new paragraph when the topic changes.

   d. Titles should be a rewording of the thesis sentence.

   e. Once you have written a first draft, you only need to correct spelling and grammar.

ANSWERS

Chapters 1–5

1. a. proper noun; **b.** pronoun; **c.** adverb modifying the adjective "wilted"; **d.** adverb modifying the verb "went"; **e.** preposition; **f.** adjective modifying "Corry"

Chapters 6 and 7

2. a. No error; **b.** Run-on sentence; **c.** Sentence fragment; **d.** Faulty parallelism

Chapters 8–10

3. a. I have labeled all the plants by kingdom and phylum <u>period</u> This will aid us in the following areas <u>colon</u> research <u>comma</u> review <u>comma</u> and <u>NP</u> presentation of our science project <u>period</u>

b. Does she know <u>comma or dash</u> although it does not really matter <u>comma or dash</u> about the reward for the lost child <u>question mark</u>

c. "Stop <u>exclamation mark</u>" she exclaimed in terror <u>period</u>

d. "This product is flammable <u>comma</u>" Erik read aloud <u>period</u>

Chapter 11

4. a. affect; **b.** Besides; **c.** It's; **d.** its; **e.** Lay; **f.** lies; **g.** their; **h.** They're

5. a. wordy; **b.** wordy; **c.** not wordy

Chapters 12 and 13

6. a. thesis; **b.** topic; **c.** topic; **d.** thesis

Chapters 14 and 15

7. a. true; **b.** false; **c.** true; **d.** false; **e.** false

CRITICAL THINKING

Review the respective chapters for information related to the following questions.

Chapter 1

1. Collective nouns do what?

2. How do you make subjects and verbs agree?

3. What is the difference between plural and possessive?

Chapter 2

4. What is an infinitive?

5. What is a gerund?

Chapter 3

6. When do you use who and when do you use whom?

Chapters 4 and 5

7. What is the difference between comparative and superlative adjectives and adverbs?

Chapter 6

8. What is the difference between an independent and a subordinate clause?

Chapter 7

9. How do you correct a run-on sentence?

10. What is a sentence fragment?

Chapter 8

11. When should you use an exclamation mark?

Chapter 9

12. When do you use a colon and when do you use a semicolon?

Chapter 10

13. Where should periods and commas be placed in relation to quotation marks?

Chapter 11

14. What are some examples of slang and clichés? Why should you avoid using them in formal written communication?

Chapters 12 and 13

15. What should you do before you start writing?

16. Why is an outline important?

17. How do you avoid plagiarism?

Chapters 14 and 15

18. What should a good introduction do?

19. What should a good conclusion do?

20. What is the purpose of revising and editing?

REAL-WORLD SCENARIOS

1. Write a persuasive essay that supports a specific position regarding the issue of capital punishment. Discuss the steps that you will take to complete this assignment.

2. How would you outline an essay for a paper about the life of Mahatma Gandhi? How would this be different from an outline for a paper that argues against gun control?

3. You can learn a lot about a new topic from one very good book. How do you decide what to quote, what to paraphrase, and what to cite in your essay?

ANSWERS

1. First, identify the purpose and audience for your writing, and narrow your topic. For example, one approach to this assignment might be to write an argument to persuade the readers of an online newsletter to support capital punishment for a specific crime. Next, write a thesis statement that makes an assertion about your topic. Then, begin researching and organizing your ideas. After researching your topic, create an outline to use as a guide. Finally, you should revise and edit, creating new drafts of your writing, to correct mistakes and improve the organization and style.

2. The purpose of the essay often dictates the organization and outline format. The essay about Gandhi is an informative essay. The traditional way to organize an informative essay about an individual's life is to move chronologically from birth to death. The gun control argument has a persuasive, not an informative, purpose. As a result, it should not be organized around a chronological history of gun control measures. A better strategy would be to organize the essay around a series of reasons or main ideas that support your position. The outlines and organization are different for the two topics because the purpose of the assignments is different.

3. Whenever you use ideas or words from another writer, you must cite the exact location where you obtained the information: in print materials (newspaper, book, journal), online (an online newsletter, Web site, or blog) from an interview, from a movie, etc. The one exception to this rule: Information considered common knowledge does not need to be identified. How do you decide? First, determine if the information you want to use in your essay is information that the average person would know. If it is not, then you must cite exactly where the information came from, even if you are not directly quoting the other author. Quotes are generally used to add support to your ideas or when the quotation is so powerful that paraphrasing it would not have the same impact. Paraphrasing is generally used to summarize or explain long passages from another author's work. Don't forget to cite the source of information that you are paraphrasing. Try to begin and end each paragraph with your own words. Then, within the paragraph, cite credible sources to support your assertions and provide additional information. Remember that this is your paper and should represent your ideas; a well-written paper is more than a series of quotations from other people.

PRACTICE PROJECTS

1. Talk to people who are good writers, and ask them what they consider to be effective writing strategies.

2. Keep copies of everything you write, and periodically review your writing to revise, edit, and improve it.

3. Ask a friend to read your writing or visit the writing center at your school to get feedback about your writing.

4. Take a writing class or keep a journal. Practice will improve your writing.

RESOURCE CENTER

The Resource Center offers the best resources available in print and online to help you study and review the core concepts of grammar, usage, and style. You can find additional resources, plus study tips and tools to help test your knowledge, at www.cliffsnotes.com.

Books About Writing

This CliffsNotes book is one of many great books about writing. If you are interested in additional resources, we suggest the following publications:

The Chicago Manual of Style: The Essential Guide for Writers, Editors and Publishers 16th Edition. University of Chicago Press, 2010. This guide has set the standard since 1909 for editing, primarily in books and periodicals (magazines, journals, newspapers).

Hale, Constance. *Sin and Syntax: How to Craft Wickedly Effective Prose.* Broadway Books, 2001. This book focuses on the relationship between grammar and style in writing.

Heffron, Jack. *The Writer's Idea Book.* Writer's Digest Books, 2002. Here you'll find numerous writing exercises to improve your confidence and your writing style.

Lamott, Anne. *Bird by Bird: Some Instructions on Writing and Life.* Anchor, 1995. This book gives readers useful and witty observations about the writing process and practical exercises to improve their writing.

Maggio, Rosalie. *How To Say It: Choice Words, Phrases, Sentences, and Paragraphs for Every Situation Third Edition.* Prentice Hall Press, 2009. This book provides some wonderful models of business and personal letters for any situation.

MLA Handbook for Writers of Research Papers Seventh Edition. Modern Languages Association, 2009. Check this handbook for answers to questions about writing a research paper on a topic in the humanities.

O'Conner, Patricia. *Words Fail Me: What Everyone Who Writes Should Know About Writing.* Mariner Books, 2009. The humorous way in which this book is written will be especially helpful for beginning writers.

Publication Manual of the American Psychological Association Sixth Edition. American Psychological Association, 2009. This is an essential reference guide for writers in the fields of behavioral and social sciences.

Sabin, William A. *The Gregg Reference Manual: Tribute Edition.* McGraw Hill Text, 2010. This is an indispensable resource for business writers.

Strunk, William, and E. B. White. *The Elements of Style 50th Anniversary Edition.* Longman, 2008. This classic guide has been popular with students and teachers for decades.

Trimble, John R. *Writing with Style Second Edition.* Prentice Hall, 1999. The author offers practical writing tips in a lively, conversational manner.

Zinsser, William. *On Writing Well: 30th Anniversary Edition.* Harper Paperbacks, 2006. This guide stresses simplicity and clarity in nonfiction writing.

Online Resources

You will find dozens of writing and grammar resources available online. Many college and university Web sites provide free, accessible grammar information, writing tips, and writing exercises. Here are a few to get you started.

www.bartleby.com/141/index.html Stop by this site for online answers to style questions based upon the guidelines outlined in *The Elements of Style* by Strunk and White.

www.dummies.com and www.wiley.com Check out these sites for more information about other books published by Wiley, Inc.

www.eslcafe.com/grammar.html This site is designed for people who are learning English as a second language.

http://grammar.about.com/ Browse subject areas ranging from sentence structure to composition. The site includes exercises and quizzes to help you improve your writing skills.

http://grammar.quickanddirtytips.com/ Listen to or read a variety of tips and hints about common grammar and writing problems. Grammar Girl is also on several social networking sites.

The following university-based Web sites provide an array of online exercises, tips, and examples—from basic grammar to writing complex research papers.

www.esc.edu/writer Empire State University College Writer's Complex

http://leo.stcloudstate.edu/ St. Cloud State University Literacy Education Online (LEO)

http://owl.english.purdue.edu/ Purdue University Online Writing Lab (OWL)

http://writing.colostate.edu/ Colorado State University

GLOSSARY

action verb   A verb that animates a sentence, either physically or mentally.

active voice   See *voice.*

additive phrase   An expression usually set off with commas that may seem to be part of the subject but is not, and therefore does not change the number of the verb.

adjective   A word that modifies a noun or pronoun.

adverb   A word that modifies a noun, pronoun, or another adverb.

adverbial clause   A subordinate clause that begins with a subordinate conjunction; it functions as an adverb within the sentence and cannot stand alone as a sentence.

agreement   See *pronoun agreement, subject-verb agreement.*

antecedent   The noun or group of words acting as a noun to which the pronoun refers.

appositive   A word or group of words that restates, describes, or identifies the noun or pronoun it follows.

audience   The reader of your writing; you should consider your audience's position and experiences when deciding on the appropriate language, style, and tone for your writing.

buzzword   A technical term that sounds important and is often used to impress; it may become a trendy word or phrase.

case   A term that refers to the way a noun or pronoun is used in a phrase, clause, or sentence; case can be subjective, objective, or possessive.

clause   A group of related words, but unlike a phrase, a clause has a subject and predicate.

clichés   Trite, overused expressions, many of which rely on figurative language and should be avoided in writing.

collective noun   A word that stands for a group of things.

colloquial   Words or phrases that are conversational, informal, or familiar expressions.

colon   Punctuation used primarily when introducing a list, a quotation, a restatement, or an explanation.

comma   The most frequently used internal punctuation in sentences; commas are used after introductory clauses and phrases, with nonrestrictive (nonessential) elements, with appositives, between items in a series, between modifiers in a series, to join independent clauses with a conjunction, and to set off interrupting elements.

comma splice   A punctuation error that occurs when a comma is used to join two independent clauses.

comparative degree   The comparative form of adjectives and adverbs used to compare two people, things, or actions.

complement (predicate nominative or predicate adjective) An element in a predicate that identifies or describes the subject; a complement can be either a noun (called a predicate noun or predicate nominative), or an adjective (called a predicate adjective).

complete predicate The verb or verb phrase and the words that modify or complete it.

complete subject The noun or pronoun and the words that modify or complete it.

complex sentence A sentence that contains one independent clause and one or more subordinate clauses.

compound adjective Two or more words that function together as a single adjective. A compound adjective is usually hyphenated when it appears before a noun.

compound adverbs Two or more words that function together as an adverb. Although most compound adverbs are written as two words, those beginning with *over* or *under* are spelled as one word.

compound-complex sentence A sentence that joins two or more independent clauses with one or more subordinate clauses.

compound preposition Prepositions made up of more than one word.

compound sentence A sentence that has two or more independent clauses, joined by coordinating conjunctions, and no subordinate clauses.

compound subject Two or more subjects that share the same verb within a sentence.

compound word Two words that, when combined, can create a spelling problem; a dictionary is the best guide for correct spelling.

conclusion The final paragraph or paragraphs that wraps up the loose ends of an essay and gives a reader a sense of completion.

conjunction A word or phrase that joins or links elements.

conjunctive (sentence) adverb A word that looks like a coordinating conjunction but actually functions as an adverb.

coordinating conjunction (*and, but, for, nor, or, so, yet*) The word that joins words, phrases, or clauses that are grammatically equal in rank.

correlative conjunction Conjunctions that come in matched pairs (like *not only/but also*).

dangling modifier A grammatical error that is similar to a misplaced modifier, except that the dangling modifier is not only separated from the word it modifies, it also is missing the word it modifies.

dash A punctuation device used to interrupt a sentence or introduce a restatement or explanation.

demonstrative pronoun (*this, that, these, those*) A pronoun that singles out what you are talking about.

direct object A noun that receives the action of the sentence but is not the subject.

draft A written version of an essay; most writers create multiple drafts for a writing project.

ellipsis   Punctuation indicating an omission from a quotation.

euphemism   A mild or roundabout word or phrase used in place of one considered painful, too strong, or offensive.

exclamation mark   Punctuation following interjections and other expressions of strong feeling; they may also lend force to a command.

faulty parallelism   A failure to create grammatically parallel structures when appropriate.

future perfect   A verb tense that indicates action in a future time in relation to another time farther in the future; it is formed with *will have* and the past participle of the verb.

future tense   A verb tense that indicates the action has yet to take place.

gerund   A noun created from the *-ing* form of a verb; a gerund acts as a subject and object in a sentence.

gerund phrase   A phrase that begins with the *-ing* form of a verb and frequently has objects and modifiers; a gerund phrase always acts as a noun in a sentence.

idiom   A phrase or expression that doesn't follow the usual patterns of language, or that has a meaning other than the literal. Expressions that have become clichés are figurative idioms.

imperative   The verb mood that is used in requests and commands.

incomplete sentence   See *sentence fragment*.

indefinite pronoun (*all, any, one, each, every, few, several,* and so on)   A pronoun that stands in for a noun but does not specify the person or thing to which it refers.

independent clause   A clause that contains a subject and a verb, expresses a complete thought, and can stand alone as a sentence.

indicative   The verb mood that is used in most statements and questions.

indirect object   The word(s) that tells to or for whom an action is done, although the words *to* and *for* are not used; it is used with a transitive verb and precedes the direct object.

indirect question   A question that is being reported rather than asked directly; it ends with a period, not a question mark.

infinitive   The base form of a verb with *to;* it usually functions as a noun, although it can be an adjective or adverb.

infinitive phrase   A phrase containing an infinitive and its objects and modifiers; infinitive phrases usually function as nouns, although they can be used as adjectives and adverbs.

intensifiers   Words intended to add force to what you say.

interjection   A word that expresses a burst of emotion but is not grammatically related to other elements in a sentence.

interrogative pronoun (*who, whom, whose, which, what*)   A pronoun that introduces a question.

intransitive verb   A verb that does not take an object.

introduction   The beginning of an essay that establishes the purpose and tone. The introduction should attract the reader's attention and establish the topic the reader will find in the rest of the paper.

irregular verb   A verb that forms the past tense and past participle in a variety of ways, but not by adding *-d* or *-ed* as regular verbs do.

jargon   The specialized language or vocabulary of a field or profession.

linking verb   A verb that does not convey action but helps complete statements about the subject by describing or identifying it.

misplaced modifier   A modifier that does not clearly relate to the word it is modifying.

modifier   A word or phrase that describes or limits another word or group of words.

mood   The manner or attitude of the speaker which the verb intends to convey; verbs have three moods: indicative, imperative, or subjunctive.

noun   A word that names a person, place, thing, idea, or activity, and can be either concrete or abstract.

noun clause   A clause that functions as a noun in a sentence.

number   A term that refers to whether a noun or verb is singular or plural.

object of the preposition   A noun or pronoun that follows a preposition and completes the prepositional phrase.

objective case   The form used for a noun or pronoun when it is the object of a verb.

outline   A tool that establishes an overall pattern of organization for an essay or paper; outlines are essential to clear, logical writing.

paragraph   A group of sentences that relate to each other as they develop an idea. Although paragraphs can vary in length, each one should focus on a single concept, which is usually stated in the topic sentence of the paragraph.

paragraph coherence   The smooth, logical flow of content in a paragraph.

parallelism   The matching of grammatical structures; elements in a sentence that have the same function or express similar ideas should be grammatically parallel, or grammatically matched.

paraphrase   The rephrasing of an idea taken from another source that the writer summarizes in his or her own words.

parentheses   Punctuation marks used to set off incidental or additional information.

participial phrase   A phrase that begins with a past or present participle and is followed by its object and modifiers; participial phrases are used as adjectives.

participle   A verb that ends in *-ing* (present participle) or *-ed, -d, -t, -en, -n* (past participle).

parts of speech   English has eight parts of speech: noun, verb, pronoun, adjective, adverb, preposition, conjunction, and interjection.

passive voice   See *voice*.

past perfect   A verb tense indicating action in past times in relation to another past time; it is formed with *had* and the past participle of the verb.

past tense   A verb tense indicating that an action is finished or completed.

period   Punctuation used with statements, requests, mild exclamations, courtesy questions, and abbreviations.

person   The term that refers to the person or thing that is a subject or object; person can be either first (*I, me, my, mine*), second (*you, your*), or third (*he, she, him, her, it, they*).

personal pronoun (*I, me, he, she, it,* and so on)   A word that stands in for one or more persons or things and differs in form depending upon its case.

phrase   A group of related words that have no subject-verb combination and cannot stand alone as a complete sentence.

plagiarism   The intentional or unintentional use of another writer's words or ideas without acknowledging the source.

possessive case   The case of a noun or pronoun used to show ownership.

predicate   The part of a sentence that tells what the subject does or is, or what is done to the subject.

preposition   A word that shows the relationship between a noun or pronoun and another word in the sentence.

prepositional phrase   A phrase that begins with a preposition and includes a noun or pronoun that is the object of the preposition.

present perfect   A verb tense that indicates action in past time in relation to present time; it is formed with *has* or *have* and the past participle of the verb.

present tense   A verb tense that indicates the action is occurring now.

pronoun   A word that stands in for a noun.

pronoun agreement   A term describing how a pronoun agrees in number (singular or plural) and gender (masculine or feminine) with its antecedent (the noun the pronoun replaces).

pronoun case   The term that refers to the way a pronoun is used in a sentence. See also *objective case, possessive case, subjective case*.

proper noun   A word(s), always capitalized, that names a specific person or place, or a particular event or group.

punctuation   The symbol that helps a reader navigate each sentence and make sense of what is written. Punctuation devices include periods, question marks, exclamation marks, commas, semicolons, colons, dashes, parentheses, and brackets.

question mark   Punctuation used to end a question.

quotation marks   Punctuation used to indicate that the words or sentences within the quotation marks are borrowed from another writer or speaker.

redundancy   Unnecessary repetition of words, phrases, or ideas in writing.

reflexive (intensive) pronoun   The pronoun form that combines a personal pronoun with *-self* or *-selves* to reflect nouns or pronouns, or to emphasize.

relative clause   A clause that begins with a relative pronoun and functions as an adjective.

relative pronoun (*who, whom, which, that*)   The pronoun form used to introduce clauses that describe nouns or pronouns.

run-on sentence   The grammatical error in which two independent clauses are joined without correct punctuation.

semicolon   Punctuation that is stronger than a comma but weaker than a colon and is most often used to join two independent clauses.

sentence   A group of words containing a subject and a predicate and expressing a complete thought.

sentence fragment   A group of words that is missing a subject, a verb, or does not express a complete thought; it is also called an incomplete sentence.

simple predicate   A verb or verb phrase that tells what the subject is or does.

simple sentence   A sentence that has one independent clause and no subordinate clauses.

simple subject   A noun or pronoun.

slang   Conversational or informal words or phrases, which should generally be avoided in formal writing.

split infinitive   An infinitive that is divided by one or more adverbs between the word "to" and the verb.

subject   The part of a sentence that tells what or whom the sentence is about.

subjective (nominative) case   The form of a noun or pronoun that is used when it is the subject of a verb.

subject-verb agreement   A term describing how a verb must agree (in person and number) with its subject, regardless of other elements or phrases that come between the subject and the verb.

subjunctive   The verb mood used in sentences that are contrary-to-fact or hypothetical.

subordinate (dependant) clause   A clause that does not express a complete thought and is not a sentence; it depends upon something else to express a complete thought.

subordinating conjunction   A conjunction that joins subordinate clauses to independent clauses.

superlative degree   The form used with adjectives and adverbs to compare more than two things, people, or actions.

tense   The term that refers to the time when the action, or state of being of the verb, is taking place.

thesis   A sentence or several sentences that make an assertion about the topic; it is usually found in the introduction and may be directly stated or implied.

topic   The general idea or theme of an essay.

transitive verb   A verb that takes a direct object; that is, the verb transmits action to an object.

verb   The word or phrase that conveys the action performed by a subject, expresses the state of that subject, or links the subject to a complement.

verb agreement   See *subject-verb agreement.*

verbal   Words derived from verbs but that function differently from a verb. See also *gerund, infinitive, participle.*

voice   The form of a verb that indicates whether the subject performs the action (active voice) or receives the action (passive voice).

wordy expression   An expression that repeats information or avoids getting directly to the point.

Appendix
FREQUENTLY CONFUSED WORDS

Choosing the right word is important, but some words are easy to confuse. Words that sound alike can be spelled differently, and words that are not acceptable usage can be mistakenly used for appropriate words. As a writer, your job is to communicate clearly. Always check a dictionary if you are uncertain about a word's meaning. Keep in mind that the meaning of a word can sometimes change over time. This appendix lists some commonly confused words that frustrate writers.

a, an: Use the article **a** before words that begin with consonant sounds and words that begin with a *"yew"* sound: *a bag, a plan, a historic treaty, a union, a one-armed man* (*one* is pronounced as if it begins with a *w*). Use **an** before words that begin with a vowel sound: *an advertisement, an hour* (the *h* is silent), *an NBC executive* (*NBC* sounds as if it begins with *e*).

a lot, alot: **A lot** is a colloquial, vague expression meaning very much or very many; avoid using the phrase *a lot* in writing. **Alot** is a misspelling of *a lot*.

a while, awhile: These words mean essentially the same thing, but there is a distinction. **While** means period of time, and therefore it is correct to write *He left for a while.* However, **awhile** means for a period of time, with the *for* as part of the definition. Therefore, it is correct to write *He waited awhile* but not *He waited for awhile.*

accept, except: **Accept** means to receive or to agree with: *I accept the gift. I accept your proposal.* **Except** as a preposition means leaving out or (as a verb) to exclude: *Everyone except you is invited. He was excepted from the requirement.*

adapt, adopt, adept: When you **adapt** something, you change it to suit a purpose, such as adapting a novel for a screenplay, or adapting yourself to a new environment. When you **adopt** something, you take it as is and make it your own. For example, the local chapter of a club may adopt its national organization's constitution. **Adept** means highly skilled, an expert. *She is an adept mountain climber.*

adverse, averse: Adverse means unfavorable. *Adverse conditions make a trip unlikely.* **Averse** means disinclined or reluctant. *The staff members are averse to taking a salary cut.*

advice, advise: Advice is a noun. *Take my advice.* **Advise** is a verb. *I advise you not to go.*

affect, effect: The most common mistake here is to confuse the verb **affect** with the noun **effect**. The verb **affect** means to influence, while the noun **effect** means result. *The decision to strike affects us all because the effect of a strike at this time will be devastating.* (If you can put *the* in front of it, the word is *effect.*) Less frequently, *effect* is used as a verb meaning to bring about, to accomplish. *Harris effected a change in company policy.* Still less frequently, and with the accent on the first syllable, *affect* is used as a noun meaning an emotion or mood as a factor in behavior or a stimulus arousing an emotion or mood. The use of *affect* as a noun is limited to the field of psychology.

aid, aide: Aid means assistance (noun) and to assist (verb). The word **aide** means a person who is an assistant. *Her aide spoke to the press.*

all ready, already: All ready means all prepared. *I am all ready to go on the picnic.* **Already** means by or before the given or implied time. *I was already aware that the plan wouldn't work.*

all right, alright: All right, meaning good or okay, is correct. *His performance was all right.* **Alright** is an incorrect spelling.

all together, altogether: All together means all at one time or in one place. *When we rescued the five men, they were all together on the ledge.* **Altogether** means completely, in all. *Altogether, we rescued five men.*

allude, refer, elude: To **allude** to something is to speak of it indirectly, without specifically mentioning it. *When he said his father was unable to care for himself, he was probably alluding to the filthy house and empty refrigerator.* To **refer** to something is to mention it directly. *He referred to the filthy house and empty refrigerator as evidence that his father couldn't live alone.* To **elude** is to escape or avoid capture. *He eluded his pursuers for a week.*

allusion, illusion, delusion: An **allusion** is an indirect reference. *When she spoke of Robert's listening to the ghost of his father, it was an allusion to Hamlet's behavior in Shakespeare's play.* An **illusion** is a false idea or unreal image. *The security system created an illusion of safety.* A **delusion** is a false belief, usually pathological. *Suffering from the delusion that he was Superman, he tried to fly.*

altar, alter: The noun **altar** is a platform used for sacred purposes, while the verb **alter** means to change. *Reverend Wolfe asked them not to alter the altar.*

alternate, alternative; alternately, alternatively: **Alternate** as an adjective means every other. *They meet on alternate Mondays.* **Alternative** means providing a choice between things. *The alternative plan is to meet on alternate Tuesdays.* As adverbs, **alternately** means one after the other, whereas **alternatively** means one or the other. *The day was alternately sunny and stormy. He could have decided to stay home or, alternatively, to dress lightly but carry a raincoat and umbrella.*

among, between: In general, use **between** for two items or people and **among** for more than two items or people. *The money was to be divided between Sophie and Jonathan. The money was to be divided among Sophie, Jonathan, and Brian. Among* suggests a looser relationship than *between.* Therefore, when three or more things are brought into a close, reciprocal relationship, such as they would be with a treaty, *between* is better than *among. The treaty between Germany, France, and Italy was never ratified.*

amount, number: **Amount** refers to a bulk or mass. *No amount of money would be enough.* **Number** refers to individual countable items. *He took a large number of stamps* not *He took a large amount of stamps.*

any one, anyone: Use **any one** when you are referring to one particular person or thing. *Any one of the three girls is qualified.* Otherwise, use **anyone.** *Anyone can pick up a free copy.*

any way, anyway, anyways: Use **any way** as an adjective-noun pair. *I can't think of any way we can lose.* **Anyway** is an adverb meaning in any case. *Our star player was sick, but we won the game anyway.* **Anyways** is incorrect, substandard usage.

avenge, revenge: To **avenge** is to punish a wrong with the idea of seeing justice done. **Revenge** is harsher and/or less concerned with justice than with retaliating by inflicting harm. *Her father avenged her death by working to have the man arrested, tried, and convicted. Her boyfriend took revenge by killing the man's wife.*

average, mean, median: Statistically, the **average** of a group of numbers is the result of dividing their sum by the number of quantities in the group. (For example, the average of 3, 4, 6, and 7 is 20 divided by 4, or 5.) Average is also used outside statistics to mean ordinary or typical. The **mean** is the same as the average. (For example, the mean temperature of a day whose low is 30 degrees and whose high is 60 degrees is 45 degrees—30 plus 60 is 90, which equals 45 when divided by 2.) The **median** is the point in a series of ascending or descending numbers where half the numbers in the series are on one side and half on the other. (For example, in the series 5, 7, 9, 12, and 16, the median is 9.)

bad, badly: Bad is an adjective modifying or describing a state of being, usually of the subject. Use *bad* after the verbs *feel* or *look*. **Badly** is an adverb describing the quality of the verb. *She felt bad that the driver of the car was injured badly.*

beside, besides: Beside means next to, at the side of. **Besides** means in addition to. *I don't want to spend my life living beside the dump. Besides its convenient office location, my new employer provides good health and retirement benefits.*

biannual, biennial: Biannual means twice a year; **biennial** means every two years.

bimonthly, biweekly: Bimonthly can mean either every two months or twice a month. **Biweekly** can mean either every two weeks or twice a week. Because of these dual meanings, it is clearer to use terms such as twice a month or every two months instead.

bloc, block: Use **block** except when referring to a coalition of people or nations. Then the word is **bloc.** *The gun-control bloc (not block) defeated the amendment.*

capital, capitol: Use **capital** when referring to the city that is the seat of a government. *The capital of California is Sacramento.* Use **capitol** when referring to the building where a legislature meets. *When we arrived there, we toured the capitol and other government buildings.*

censor, censure: To **censor** something is to edit, remove, or prohibit it because it is judged objectionable. To **censure** someone is to strongly condemn him or her as wrong. *The vice principal censured the class president for her fiery speech, but he didn't censor the text of her speech.*

cite, site, sight: Cite is a verb meaning to summon before a court of law, to mention by way of example, or to officially mention as meritorious. *I am citing you for creating a public nuisance. The young officer was cited for bravery.* **Site** is a noun meaning location or scene. *We drove quickly to the site of the accident.* **Sight** is also a noun, meaning the ability to see or something seen. *From the hill, the stormy ocean was a beautiful sight.*

compare to, compare with; contrast to, contrast with: To **compare** things means to describe their similarities, differences, or both. To **contrast**

means to point out differences only. Use **compare to** when stating a likeness between things. *The final scene in the novel can be compared to the final scene in the play, since both show a reconciliation of opposing forces.* Use **compare with** when showing similarities, differences, or both. *Compared with what was budgeted for prisons, the amount budgeted for crime prevention was small, but both amounts were increased from last year.* Use **contrast to** when showing things with opposite characteristics. *The Garcias' peaceful marriage is in contrast to the Nelsons' bitter relationship.* Use **contrast with** when juxtaposing things to illustrate their differences. *They contrasted Mr. Headley's plan for bringing in new businesses with Ms. Friedman's proposal.*

complement, compliment: As a noun, **complement** means something that completes or perfects something else, and, as a verb, to accompany or complete something else. *His creativity was the perfect complement to her determination. The dessert complemented the dinner.* **Compliment** as a noun means something said in praise, and as a verb to praise. *Her compliment about his dancing pleased him; he in turn complimented her on her gracefulness.*

compose, comprise: **Compose** means to make up. *Two senators from each state compose the U.S. Senate.* **Comprise** means to include. *The U.S. Senate comprises two senators from each state.* The most common mistake is to use *comprise* for *compose.* Remember that the whole comprises the parts, not the other way around. Also, don't use the phrase "is comprised of."

conscience, consciousness: **Conscience** is an inner voice, a sense of right and wrong; whereas **consciousness** is simply awareness, or the ability to think and feel. *Consciousness of the woman's plight didn't seem to bother his conscience.* The adjectival forms are **conscientious,** which means scrupulous, painstaking, or acting in accordance with conscience; and **conscious,** which means awake or aware.

contemptible, contemptuous: **Contemptible** means deserving contempt, while **contemptuous** means showing or feeling contempt. *We were contemptuous of their feeble explanation for their contemptible behavior toward the animals.*

continual, continuous: Something that is **continual** is repeated often. Something that is **continuous** goes on without interruption. *I made continual requests for a seat change because of the baby's continuous crying.*

council, counsel: **Council,** a noun, is a committee or an administrative body. **Counsel** as a noun is advice, an exchange of ideas, or a lawyer or group of lawyers. *Her counsel advised her that she should first seek counsel* *from an expert and then approach the town council. Council* is never a verb. *Counsel* as a verb means to give advice. *She counseled him to increase his investments in the stock market.*

denote, connote: Denote refers to the dictionary definition of a word. *The noun "rose" denotes a particular flower.* **Connote** means what a word may imply or suggest. For example, the noun *rose* can *connote* youth, beauty, the impermanence of beauty, freshness, etc. *Connotations* include all the suggestions and nuances that are beyond a word's dictionary definition.

device, devise: A device (noun) is an instrument, either something concrete like a can opener or something abstract like a plan. **Devise,** a verb, means to create or fashion a device. *They devised an ingenious device for pitting olives.*

different from, different than: When comparing two things, use **different from:** *The movie is different from* (not *than*) *the book. My goals are different from* (not *than*) *yours.* If *different* introduces a subordinate clause, use the subordinating conjunction **than.** *The true story was different than I had believed.*

dilemma, problem: Don't use **dilemma** to mean problem. A **dilemma** means a choice between two unattractive alternatives. *Her dilemma was whether to put up with her neighbor's noise or to give up the inexpensive apartment.* A **problem** doesn't necessarily involve such a choice. *The problem of how to provide universal health care plagued us,* not *The dilemma of how to provide universal health care plagued us.*

discreet, discrete: If you are **discreet** you are careful about what you do and say; you show prudence and good judgment. **Discrete,** however, means separate and distinct. *It was discreet of the maid to divide the laundry into discrete piles, one of Rebecca's clothes and one of Toni's.*

disinterested, uninterested: Disinterested means impartial, and **uninterested** means lacking interest. A jury that is *disinterested* is desirable; a jury that is *uninterested* is not, because the members may doze off during the trial.

e.g., i.e.,: The abbreviation **e.g.** (from the Latin *exempli gratia*) means *for example.* Do not confuse it with the abbreviation **i.e.** (from the Latin *id est*), which means *that is (to say).*Use *e.g.* when you are citing some but not all examples. *He took camping equipment with him, e.g., a tent, a cooking stove, and a sleeping bag.* Do not use *etc.* with *e.g.* because the idea of more examples than are being cited is already present in *e.g.* Use *i.e.* when you are presenting an equivalent of the preceding term. *He will study the document, i.e., the committee's official confirmation.* In a formal essay you should write out *for example* and *that is* rather than using the abbreviations.

emigrate, immigrate: When you leave a country, you **emigrate** from it. When you come into a country, you **immigrate** to it. *His parents, who emigrated from Russia, immigrated to the United States.*

eminent, imminent, emanate: Eminent means prominent, while **imminent** means about to happen. *The eminent lawyer was in imminent danger of being shot.* **Emanate** means to issue from a source. *A ghostly light emanated from the cloud.*

entitled, titled: Use **entitled** to mean the right to have or do something. *The Doyles were entitled to the money.* Do not use it to mean **titled.** *The book is titled* (not *entitled*) The Habitats of Wolves.

envelop, envelope: Envelop is a verb meaning to cover completely or surround. *The fog enveloped the town.* **Envelope** is a noun meaning something that covers, such as an envelope for a letter.

envy, jealousy: Although sometimes used synonymously, *envy* and *jealousy* have different meanings. **Envy** is the desire for something that someone else has, or a feeling of ill will over another's advantages. *My envy of your success has made me bitter.* **Jealousy** is a resentful suspicion that someone else has what rightfully belongs to the jealous person. *Out of jealousy, he followed his wife. By favoring their daughter, they created jealousy in their son.*

et al., etc.: The abbreviation **et al.** (Latin *et alit*) means *and others.* It, rather than *etc.*, should be used to refer to additional people. *The research paper was prepared by S. Robinson, F Lupu, I Alderson, et al.* Use this abbreviation only in bibliographical entries or similar citations. The abbreviation **etc.** (Latin *et cetera*) also means *and others,* but it is used with things, not people. *Don't forget to collect test papers, pencils, scratch pads, etc.* If you use the phrase *such as* before a list of items, don't use *etc. Gym equipment, such as basketballs, nets, and towels, will be provided* not *Gym equipment, such as basketballs, nets, towels, etc., will be provided.*

every one, everyone: Every one means each one of a group of items or people. *Every one of those people who came to the party early left drunk.* **Everyone** means all, everybody. *Everyone who left the party was drunk.*

farther, further: Use **farther** in referring to physical distance. *I walked farther than you.* Otherwise, use **further.** *I will question the suspect further.*

faze, phase: Faze is a verb meaning to disturb or daunt; **phase** is a noun meaning a period or stage: *This phase of her son's behavior didn't faze her.* As a verb, *phase* (with *in*) means to introduce or carry out in stages. *They phased in the new equipment at the plant.*

fewer, less: Use **fewer** for individual countable items or people; use **less** for bulk, degree, or quantity. *We expected fewer* (not *less*) *people to come. Climbing the mountain took less effort* (not *fewer*) *than we thought.*

flair, flare: If you have a **flair** for something, you have a natural talent for it. *Her flair for putting people at ease impressed us.* A **flare** is a flame or bright light. *Flare* as a verb means to blaze brightly or burst out suddenly. *Flair* is never a verb.

flaunt, flout: Flaunt means to make a gaudy or defiant display of something. It is sometimes confused with **flout,** which means to scorn or mock. *He flouted* (not *flaunted*) *convention by wearing jeans to the black-tie dinner. She flaunted* (not *flouted*) *her new company car in front of her coworkers.*

fortunate, fortuitous: Fortunate means lucky, having good fortune. Fortuitous means happening by chance. A **fortuitous** event isn't necessarily favorable. *It was merely fortuitous that she was standing on the trail when the landslide began, but she was fortunate enough to escape injury.*

forward, foreword: Forward means ahead, or at or toward the front. **Foreword** is an introduction at the beginning of a book.

fulsome, abundant: Don't use *fulsome* when you mean **abundant** (profuse or great quantity). **Fulsome** means excessive or offensive. Therefore, receiving *fulsome* praise for an action is not something to be happy about, while receiving *abundant* praise is.

gamut, gauntlet: Gamut means the entire range or extent. *His reactions ran the gamut from rage to apathy.* Don't confuse this word with *gauntlet.* **Gauntlet** has two meanings. First, it refers to a glove which in the days of chivalry was thrown to the ground to announce a challenge. Therefore, *throwing down the gauntlet* has become a figure of speech meaning to challenge. *A fifty-year-old woman entered the race, thus throwing down the gauntlet to the younger runners.* Second, *gauntlet* was also once a form of punishment in which a person ran between two rows of men who struck him. It has also become a figure of speech. *In trying to promote her idea, she was forced to run the gauntlet between those who thought it was too ambitious and those who thought it wasn't ambitious enough.*

grisly, grizzly: A crime is **grisly** (ghastly, terrifying); **grizzly** is a type of bear, or someone whose hair is partially gray. *Meeting a grizzly bear in the woods could be a grisly experience.*

hanged, hung: Although the usual past tense and past participle of hang is **hung, hanged** is still preferred when referring to people. *We hung the paintings yesterday* but *They hanged the murderer last week.*

historic, historical: If something is **historic,** it figures in history. If something is **historical,** it pertains to history. Betsy Ross's home is a *historic* building; the moon landing is a *historic* event. On the other hand, you may take a *historical* tour of Washington D.C., read a *historical* novel, or buy a book of *historical* maps.

implicit, tacit, explicit: Implicit means implied or unstated; however, it can also mean without reservation, which sometimes causes confusion. In a statement such as *The consequences of the action were implicit in the letter,* it is obvious that the meaning is implied. But the meaning is ambiguous in this statement: *Their trust in the committee was implicit.* Does *implicit* mean the trust was implied rather than stated, or does it mean the trust was beyond question? It would be clearer to say either *Their trust in the committee was left implicit* (unstated) or *Their trust in the committee was absolute.* **Tacit** means unspoken, not expressed openly, and is similar to one of the meanings of *implicit. Tacit* refers to speech rather than general expression. *Although he didn't specifically address her, his speech gave her the tacit approval she needed to continue her project.* **Explicit,** the opposite of *implicit,* means clearly stated. *The professor was explicit in presenting the course requirements.*

imply, infer: Imply means to suggest something indirectly. **Infer** means to conclude from facts or indications. *If I imply by yawning that I'm tired, you might infer that I want you to leave.* Think of *implying* as done by the actor, *inferring* as done by the receiver. The most common error is to use *infer* when *imply* is correct. *To influence the buyer, the owner implied* (not *inferred*) *that the property would increase in value within a few months. All the reports implied* (not *inferred*) *that the death was a suicide.*

incredible, incredulous: Incredible means unbelievable or so astonishing as to seem unbelievable, whereas **incredulous** means skeptical or unbelieving: *We were incredulous as we listened to his incredible story about being abducted by aliens.* Avoid the colloquial (imprecise) overuse of *incredible* to mean striking or very, as in *That's an incredible dress you're wearing* or *I was incredibly sad.*

inflammable, flammable: Inflammable and **flammable** both mean easily set on fire, will burn readily. Because people might think *inflammable* means not easily set on fire (as *inactive* means not active, *incoherent* means not coherent, etc.), those who deal with fires and fire safety argue that flammable should be used for warning signs and labels.

irregardless, regardless: Although **irregardless** is widely used, it is never correct. The word should be **regardless.** *Regardless of what you think, the changes will be made.*

its, it's: Its is the possessive of *it: The tree lost its leaves.* **It's** is a contraction of *it is: It's too bad we can't come.*

lay, lie: These verbs cause trouble for many people. If you mean *recline,* use **lie.** If you mean *set, place,* or *put,* use **lay.** An easy way to remember which one to use is to recognize that *lie* does not take an object and *lay* does: *I lie down for a nap every day. The dog lies by the fire. I lay the paper on the table. Chickens lay eggs.* The past tense and the past participles of *lie* are *lay* and *lain. I lay down for a nap yesterday. I have lain down every afternoon this week.* The past and past participle of *lay* are *laid* and *laid. I laid the paper on the table yesterday. I have laid it in the same spot for years.*

lead, led (verbs): **Led** is the past tense of **lead.** *Last week he led the choir rehearsal; I usually lead the choir, but I was ill.*

like, as: Both **as** and **like** can be used as prepositions. *He sleeps like a baby. We see this as an alternative.* But only *as* is a subordinating conjunction; so when you are introducing a clause, don't use *like. The storm started after lunch, just as* (not *like*) *I said it would.* Do not use *like* to refer to speaking, thinking, or a state of being. *And I'm like, "It's okay with me."*

lightning, lightening: Lightning is a flash of light. **Lightening** means becoming lighter.

literally, figuratively: Literally means true to the meaning of the words, or precisely as stated. It is often misused to mean almost or definitely, as in *I literally died when he chose me.* If you literally died, you would be talking from beyond the grave. In the sentence *I literally died when he chose me, died* is being used not literally but **figuratively,** as a metaphor for the overwhelming reaction you experienced. To convey this emotion you could say, *I almost died when he chose me.* Use *literally* only when referring to the meaning precisely as stated. *By blocking the door, he literally refused to let anyone leave the room. The literal subject of the poem is the flowers, but the poet is using them figuratively to represent the impermanence of beauty.*

loath, loathe: Loath is an adjective meaning reluctant. **Loathe** is a verb meaning to despise. *I am loath to admit that I loathe David.*

lose, loose: Lose means to be unable to find. **Loose,** an adjective, means unrestrained or inexact. *I often lose the loose change I keep in my pocket. The poem loses its power in such a loose translation. Loose* is used less frequently as a verb. It means to set free or make less tight. *She loosed the bird into the air. He loosed* (more commonly, *loosened*) *the victim's clothing.*

much, many: Much is a noun meaning large in number, size, or quantity. *We have much to get done before 5:00.* **Many** is an adjective indicating a large, indefinite number. *Many students wait to begin their research until the night before a paper is due.*

nauseated, nauseous: When you're sick to your stomach, you're **nauseated.** The thing that made you sick—for example, rotten meat—is **nauseous.** Twirling the baby and throwing him up in the air makes him *nauseated* (not *nauseous*). The baby would be *nauseous* only if the sight of him made someone else feel *nauseated.*

oral, verbal, written: Oral means uttered, spoken. **Verbal** means of, in, or by means of words, whether the words are spoken or written. An *oral* agreement is an unwritten agreement. A *verbal* agreement can be either a spoken or written agreement. To avoid confusion, use *oral* or *written* instead of the ambiguous *verbal.* Reserve *verbal* for situations in which you are distinguishing communication in words from other types of communication, such as sign language and body movements.

passed, past: Passed is a verb. *I passed the test. We passed the old barn on our way here.* **Past** is either a noun, an adjective, or a preposition—but never a verb *The past haunts us. His past sins caught up with him. We drove past the frozen lake.*

people, person: Use **people** rather than **persons** to refer to a group of human beings. *I wish more people appreciated his artwork. He picked four people* (not *four persons*) *for the management team.* Use **person** to refer to one human being. *She is a person of integrity.* A group of people sharing a culture can be referred to as *a people. The Lakota are a people of the plains.*

personal, personnel: Personal means private or individual; **personnel** pertains to staff, workers, a company's employees. *The human resources director must keep some personal contact information about all company personnel.*

precede, proceed: Precede means to go before in time, place, rank, etc. *His remarks preceded the musical program.* **Proceed** means to move forward.

Before we proceed, we should be sure of the rules. Since the meaning of *proceed* includes the idea of moving forward, don't use it as a fancy word for *go*, particularly in situations when the movement isn't forward. *They went back* (or *returned*) *to the car,* not *They proceeded back to the car.*

principal, principle: Principal as an adjective means first in importance. As a noun, **principal** means the head of a school. *The principal reason that Mrs. Nelson was chosen to be principal of our school was her dedication.* **Principle** is a noun meaning a fundamental truth or law upon which others are based, or a rule of conduct. *The principal's principles were questioned by the parent group.*

prone, supine: If you are **prone,** you are lying face downward. If you are **supine,** you are lying face upward.

prostate, prostrate: The **prostate** is a male gland. **Prostrate,** an adjective, means lying prone or overcome. *He has recovered from prostate cancer* but *She was prostrate from the heat.*

ravage, ravish: Ravage means to destroy violently or to devastate, while **ravish** means to abduct, to rape, or to transport with joy or delight. *The troops ravaged* (not *ravished*) *all the cities they entered. The villain ravished* (not *ravaged*) *the beautiful maiden. The soprano's voice ravished* (not *ravaged*) *his ears and left him smiling.*

rebut, refute: The common error is to use *refute* for *rebut.* When you **rebut** an opponent's argument, you speak or write against it. When you **refute** an argument, you actually disprove it. Whether you have *refuted* your opponent's argument is often a matter of opinion. Avoid using it loosely. *The government spokesperson rebutted* (not *refuted*) *the argument that the war on drugs had been a disaster.*

regretfully, regrettably: Regretfully means filled with regret. Don't use it in place of **regrettably,** which means in a manner that calls for regret. *Regrettably* (not *regretfully*), *the militia was too late to save the small village. The soldiers watched regretfully as the buildings burned.*

reticent, reluctant: Don't use **reticent** as a synonym for **reluctant.** *Reticent* means disinclined to speak, not just disinclined or unwilling (*reluctant*): *The group was reticent about its reluctance to admit new members.*

sit, set: Sit usually doesn't take an object: *I sit down.* **Set** usually takes an object. *I set the book down.* Don't use them interchangeably. *Set* (not *Sit*) *that load down and sit* (not *set*) *down and talk to me.* **Sit** can take an object when it means to cause to sit, to seat. *I sat the toddler in the high chair and called the doctor.* **Set** doesn't take an object when it means to become firm

(*Let the cement set overnight*); to begin to move (*We set forth yesterday*); or to sink below the horizon (*The sun sets*).

some time, sometime, sometimes: Some time is a span of time: *Some time passed before she came in.* **Sometime** means at an unspecified time. *He said we should get together sometime.* **Sometimes** means at times. *Sometimes I'm so nervous I can't sleep.*

stationary, stationery: Stationary means still, at rest; **stationery** is paper. Think of writing letters (spelled with an *e*) on stationery (also spelled with an *e*).

tack, tact: One meaning of the noun **tack** is a course of action or policy, especially one differing from a preceding course. *He decided to take a different tack.* A common mistake is to use the noun *tact* in such contexts. **Tact** usually means sensitivity and skill in dealing with people, or diplomacy.

than, then: Don't use **then** (which means at that time) in comparisons. Use **than:** *He is wiser than* (not *then*) *his father was then.*

their, there, they're: Their is the possessive form of *they;* **there** usually refers to a place or is used in impersonal constructions (*there is, there are*); **they're** is a contraction of *they are.* Notice the correct uses of these words in the following sentence: *There is no question that their friends live there and that they're willing to help.*

themselves, theirselves: Themselves, which is an emphatic form of *them,* is correct, as in, *The producers themselves left the movie theater.* **Theirselves** is not acceptable usage.

to, too: To has several meanings, the first being *toward.* **Too** means also or more than enough. *I walked to the river, which was too wild for me to swim in. My father thought so too.*

tortuous, torturous: Tortuous means full of twists and turns: a tortuous mountain road, a tortuous plot. **Torturous** means severely painful, agonizing. *Enduring the hot, dry trek across the Sahara was torturous.*

toward, towards: American usage is **toward; towards** is used in Britain.

usage, use, utilize: Usage means established practice. Don't use it as a substitute for the noun **use.** *Use* (not *Usage*) *of gloves is recommended.* A common tendency is to replace the verb *use* with **utilize** and the noun *use* with **utilization** to make the verb sound more important. This inflation is not recommended. *We want to use* (not *utilize*) *our assets wisely. Use* (not *Utilization*) *of old equipment has become a major problem.*

waive, wave: The correct expression is to waive one's rights, not to wave one's rights. **Waive** means to relinquish; **wave** means move to and fro.

weather, whether: **Weather** is the state of the atmosphere; **whether** means *if.*

whose, who's: **Whose** is the possessive of *who.* **Who's** is a contraction of *who is. Who's going to tell me whose jacket this is?*

your, you're: **Your** is the possessive of *you.* **You're** is a contraction of *you are: You're certain this is your jacket?*

INDEX

introductions
  overview, 175
  suggestions for, 176–178
  what to avoid, 175–176
introductory adverbial clauses, 111–112
introductory clauses, using commas after, 111–112
introductory phrases, 111–112
irregardless, regardless, 224
irregular verbs, 25–27
"it is" expressions, 144
its, it's, 224

J

jargon
  avoiding, 139
  chapter questions, 146–147
  defined, 135
  negative connotations of, 139
  overview, 139
jealousy, envy, 221
joining independent clauses, 80, 119
joint ownership in possessive nouns, 7

L

Lamott, Anne
  Bird by Bird: Some Instructions on Writing and Life, 203
language checklist, 192
lay, lie, 224
layout of final draft, 190
lead, led, 224
led, lead, 224
length of paragraphs, 178–179
LEO (St. Cloud State University Literacy Education Online), 205
less, fewer, 222
lie, lay, 224
lightening, lightning, 224
lightning, lightening, 224
like, as, 224
linking verbs
  overview, 11–13
  using adjectives after, 49–50
literally, figuratively, 224
loath, loathe, 225
logic fallacies, 155
loose, lose, 225
lose, loose, 225

M

Maggio, Rosalie
  How To Say It: Choice Words, Phrases, Sentences, and Paragraphs for Every Situation Third Edition, 203

main idea, identifying, 156
many, much, 225
mean, median, average, 217–218
median, average, mean, 217–218
misplaced modifiers, 88–89
misplaced participial phrases, 89–90
mixing clichés, 138
MLA Handbook for Writers of Research Papers Seventh Edition (Modern Languages Association), 203
modifiers. *See also* adjectives; adverbs
  dangling, 90–91
  misplaced, 88–89
  overview, 47–48
  placement in sentences, 88–91
  using commas between, 116–117
  when to use, 48–51
moods of verbs, 20–22
most, almost, 51
much, many, 225

N

name-calling, 155
narrative essays, 164–165
nauseated, nauseous, 225
nauseous, nauseated, 225
nonrestrictive elements, using commas with, 113–114
note taking, 160
noun clauses, 71–72
nouns
  agreement with verbs, 7–8
  chapter questions, 9
  collective, 5, 44
  defined, 3
  plural, 6
  possessive case of, 6–7
  proper, 3–4
  singular, 6
  verbs used as, 4–5
numbers, 16, 42–44, 217

O

objective case
  defined, 34
  of pronouns, 36–39
O'Conner, Patricia
  Words Fail Me: What Everyone Who Writes Should Know About Writing, 204
"of" construction, 7
On Writing Well: 30th Anniversary Edition (Zinsser), 204
online practice questions, 2
online resources, 204–205
oral, verbal, written, 225

NOTES

NOTES

NOTES

NOTES